GETTING IT WRITE

Common sense copywriting for your business

NOT SO MUCH A *HOW TO* BOOK,

MORE OF A *WHY NOT LOOK AT IT THIS WAY?*

GETTING IT WRITE

www.createcommunication.co.uk -
talk@createcommunication.co.uk
0208 421 3328 - 0788 799 5749

create communication
COPYWRITING

Text copyright @ November 2017

Marilyn Messik

All Rights Reserved by

Marilyn Messik

Published by Satin Publishing

Cover design and photography: Gail D'Almaine

ISBN-13: 978-1981243327
ISBN-10: 1981243321

Author Biography

A regular feature and fiction writer for a variety of national magazines, Marilyn Messik set up a children's book and party business in the early '80s, opening first one shop and then another. At the end of the '80s following a trip to the U.S., she moved into the travel market, specialising in places to stay in the six New England States.

As her advisory, planning and booking service continued to flourish and grow, she concurrently set up a publishing company to make the information more widely available. *U.S. Welcome Selected Hotels & Inns* was a lush, full colour guide to boutique hotels, country inns and B&Bs, which eventually grew to take in unique accommodation all over America as well as featuring museums, galleries and historic sites. The popularity of the book on both sides of the Atlantic led to invitations to speak at industry conferences, and Marilyn served as a Board Member of the Professional Association of Innkeepers and was made an honorary member of the New England Innkeepers Association for her work in promoting the area.

As a niche company, marketing and promotional budgets were tight, but strategic alliances with far larger organisations such as North West Airlines, Johansens and the Debenhams Group offered opportunities to reach optimum numbers of targeted consumers. *Selected Hotels & Inns* was bought out by Thomas Cook Publishing.

In 2007 Marilyn set up a copywriting consultancy, **Create Communication**, to work with businesses of all types and sizes, helping shape their messages to optimum effect. She's a serial networker and speaker, holds communication and creative writing workshops, has written the series of *Little Black Business Books* and is the author of three paranormal thrillers.

Her work is based on a feet-on-the-floor philosophy, planning for the best, unsurprised by the unexpected, because success depends on adaptability.

Fiction
Relatively Strange
Even Stranger
Witch Dust
Paperbacks or ebooks
http://marilynmessik.co.uk/

Non-Fiction
Little Black Business Books
ebooks
http://createcommunication.co.uk/little-black-business-books/

AUTHOR LINKS:

Twitter:	@marilyn_messik
Facebook:	marilyn.messik.5
Linkedin:	createcommunication
email:	Marilyn@createcommunication.co.uk
Website:	www.createcommunication.co.uk

Publisher Links:

Satin Publishing:

http://www.satinpaperbacks.com

http://www.satinpublishing.co.uk

https://twitter.com/SatinPaperbacks

https://www.facebook.com/Satinpaperbacks.com

Email: nicky.fitzmaurice@satinpaperbacks.com

Table of Contents:

Introduction

I'm going to lay my cards flat on the table at this early stage of our acquaintance and confess, like the Tower of Pisa, I tend to lean a little towards the pessimistic. But don't get me wrong, if you're coming on this reading and writing journey with me - and I sincerely hope you will - you should know, that whilst cynical about a lot of things, I do utterly and completely believe in business success and the bigger, the brighter, the better!

I also wholeheartedly believe though that success in any arena comes from learning to trust your own common sense and gut instincts, and never religiously following a path mapped out by someone else who thinks they know better than you.

When it comes to this book, you'll find that rather than being a step by step *How To* it's more of a *Why Not Look at This Way?* sort of an effort. It's based on more years of writing for and building businesses than I care to remember - scars, T-shirt and cynicism as proof.

There's never an approach to anything that suits everyone, and writing's no exception. What works splendidly for someone else might not tick any of your boxes, so there are no absolute rights, wrongs or rules as to how to do it, just lots of options, opinions and suggestions. Some will make sense to you and nestle in like long-lost loves, others won't, and I don't think you should ever try to mould yourself to methods of working, just because someone else says it's right. If it feels wrong for you, it probably is. Relying on your own instinct rather than someone else's is far safer, usually pushes you in the right direction and on the odd occasion it doesn't – well that's just life, isn't it?

So, you can't say you haven't been warned, this book on Writing for Businesses has its feet planted very firmly on the floor, and if you're still with me and not hysterically pressing the delete button or chucking this to the other side of the room, let's move smoothly and swiftly, onwards and upwards.

Chapter One: Copywriting is . . .

The creating and writing of text, to pass information from one party to other parties, and we're not talking celebrations or politics.

Text can be long, or it can be brief - pages and pages or just one or two lines, but it isn't successful unless it conveys exactly what it's meant to convey. The complications of doing that are, oddly enough, precisely illustrated by the term copywriter. No, don't laugh. It's OK when written down, but introduced to someone who asks what I do, and they very often want to know how they go about registering a trademark or applying for a patent.

The difference between copywriting and copyrighting, exposes just what a pesky undertaking this whole communication lark can be.

Humps, Lumps and Bumps

Conveying information, like life in general, isn't as straightforward as we'd prefer. Along the way there can be a variety of unexpected humps, lumps and bumps over which you can come a cropper. But, forewarned is forearmed, and a common-sense approach and demystifying of the whole process can often prevent you falling flat on your face. The more prepared you are, the more likely to spot a bump in the distance and the easier to smoothly skirt around it.

What you write is important, but equally important is the voice with which you write. Any interaction, spoken or written is enhanced when you're likeable. And whilst lots of people might disagree with me (and lots of people usually do!) I'd suggest likeability is the most important factor in your writing. Of course, what you're saying needs to be accurate, not misspelt and within shouting distance of the rules of grammar, but the *way* you say it is vital.

In my own working life, I need to write with a lot of different voices because text I'm producing may be for a buzzy, young, innovative advertising agency in Shoreditch, an eminent Oxford research scientist, a funeral director, a government organisation or a shop selling fancy-dress costumes. And naturally, whilst fun and funny can work for fancy-dress, and wild and whacky might go down a storm with potential ad agency clients, a government or research report is going to want to be a lot less entertaining.

Whatever you're writing about, whoever you're writing it for, your text should always be likeable, not pompous and never patronising. People don't analyse text too closely, life's too short for that, but we do all know whether we get a good feeling from reading something or whether it leaves us cold and any piece that leaves you cold, isn't successful writing.

Never choose chilly, dump dull and avoid arrogant.

Chapter Two: But I Can't Write!

Oh, yes, you can, but you can only go with the flow, and if the flow isn't flowing on that day then try again tomorrow.

This is a brief chapter, because brief's the answer I give when people tell me they can't write. Truth of the matter is if you can talk and manage to make yourself understood – most of the time – then you're reasonably articulate, and writing something down isn't a whole lot different from saying it aloud. When people declare (and indeed firmly believe) they can't write, what they're actually saying is they lack the confidence to put something on paper or screen because they're scared of judgement and criticism.

Well, I hate criticism as much as the next woman (probably a darn sight more, and that's a character flaw we won't even go into right now), but if you think you're not 'good at writing', isn't it just possible you might simply be holding on to comments made back in the day – the school day? The sad fact is, one humiliating experience in front of the class, one scathing remark from a teacher can effectively put a mind-block in place for life.

Bad for the Bard

My advice is kick to the curb any block that's in your path or your past, screw your courage to the sticking point and if you've got something to say, say it, you can always edit and refine it later. And never forget, when writing about your own business your excitement, enthusiasm and authenticity is almost certainly going to come across. Your work doesn't have to be Shakespearian, in fact, if William S. found himself writing for today's short-span attentions and business purposes, he'd be right up the creek without a paddle. People want and expect to get information quickly, clearly and cleanly and aren't inclined to scroll through reams of text, however lyrically written, to achieve that.

The trickiest part of course, is putting it out there for the scrutiny of others. It's invariably at this point that what, up until now, you've viewed in a rather fond and favourable light, suddenly reads like the biggest load of twaddle anyone, anywhere, at any time has produced. Not to worry, and you're going to have to take my word for it, this perception is shared by everyone who puts words together, however skilled and experienced they may be.

Belts and Braces

On the purely practical side of things, careful proofreading of your work is highly recommended, nothing lets you down quite as badly as a typo or a misspelling. You should know though that however meticulously, indeed obsessively compulsively, any piece of text is checked, double checked and flipping-well checked again, one or two malignant little typos will have wormed their wily way in. The little sods will have lain low, only jumping up and sticking out like sore thumbs once the text has gone online or to print. If I sound a little paranoid on the subject well, that's what years of experience does to you.

My suggestion, for what it's worth, is getting whatever you've written, whether for website, blog, brochure or even a business card, checked by someone else. This won't necessarily eliminate the problem, but will at least give you another person to blame apart from yourself, which always make you feel slightly better.

Bikes and Emergency Measures

I'd very much like at this point to perk you up and say that, like riding a bike, writing gets smoother and easier the more you do it. Unfortunately, I can't, and I've already promised I won't pull the wool over your eyes, so I won't. There's no doubt there are good days when the words arrive, not only on time but in the right order and the writing flows as blissful and serene as a clear stream rippling silkily over small pebbles. There are other days which are not so good. On a not so good day, you'll spend an inordinate amount of time staring at a blank computer screen which will stare blankly right back at you. Your fingers will be poised, ready to pour forth perfect prose, but it just isn't happening. You've got nothing, nil, nada, the cupboard's bare.

Quite frankly if it's that sort of a day, there's no point fighting it. If, after taking some emergency measures – strong coffee, several chocolate biscuits and a brief banging of your head against the nearest wall – it still isn't coming, then you've no alternative but to accept that. Walk away, go do something useful and whatever you do, don't go all drama queen. It doesn't mean you can't write, it simply means you can't write today. Tomorrow may be a completely different story.

Writing blocks are like building blocks,
sooner or later you'll knock them down.

Chapter Three: Who The Heck Are You?

Grabbing someone's interest is recommended, anything more physical is not!

There are two questions you need to answer before you knuckle down to business writing, or indeed to communication of any kind;

- *Who Am I?*

- *Who Am I Talking To?*

If you don't have the answers to those two questions clear in your head, you don't have a hope in hell of communicating in the way you should. There will, of course, be occasions in your hectic life when quite frankly you're really not sure who you are, where you are, who you're talking to or indeed which way is up. At times like these, and they happen to all of us, trust me, it's best to stay as far away as possible from computers, tablets, phones, social media of any kind and probably other people.

However, on a day when you're reasonably well-adjusted and as much in control of things as you can hope to be, you shouldn't hesitate to start writing. You should write with the answers to the above two questions foremost in your mind, and you should write the same way you talk, because who you are is every bit as important as whatever business, product or service you're offering. Authenticity is worth its weight in gold and together with belief in yourself and what you're selling, can move mountains. Whilst you may have any number of doubts and uncertainties about your abilities in other areas (don't we all?), the one thing you do know better than anyone else is your own business – it's your baby and your area of expertise.

When you're writing or talking about what you do, let the enthusiasm show and never be afraid of letting your personality and individuality shine through too. You're the part of your business that's unique. People can duplicate what you do, they can copy what you say, but they can't ever be you.

You are your own unique selling point.

Chapter Four: Steer Clear Of Patchwork Quilts

You'll know when you find the voice and style that are right for you, because they'll slip on as if tailor-made.

Few, if any of us, operate in a field where we have no competition and there's usually a lot of it. But if people warm to you, if they like the sound of you and what you have to say, you'll draw them in. By the same token, if they instantly take against you, dislike what you're saying and the way you're saying it, they'll steer well clear which means, quite frankly, you'll both probably be far better off. Client relationships are no different from any other kind, they can be complicated, and it helps an awful lot if you both like each other in the first place.

Who you are is what makes your business or service different. When people tell me, they've looked through loads of competitors' websites, picked out lots of bits they like and want to incorporate in their own information, I do my best to talk them out of it. If you pick out elements of other people's sites and their style of conveying what they want to say, there's the risk that you're going to end up with an information and personality patchwork quilt which is going to do you no favours whatsoever. Your information will look, and sound cobbled together, because that's exactly what's happened.

Obviously, you'll want to look at competitors' sites to see how they talk about and tackle things, and it's always a good idea to get an idea of charges and whether or how they put them out there. But at the end of the day, your writing, your approach, the way you want to come across needs to be uniquely yours and yours alone.

Keep Calm and Clarify

Do you really know what your business or service is? I know that sounds like a truly daft and slightly insulting question, I can see you raising eyes to heaven and muttering 'duh!', but *knowing* what you do isn't at all the same thing as *communicating* it accurately.

Reflect, for just one a moment, on the number of times you've met someone at a networking or similar gathering. In response to your polite inquiry they've told you what their business is, you've nodded enthusiastically, smiled and walked away, none the wiser. They obviously must know what they do, but they've spectacularly failed to communicate that clearly to you. That's precious time wasted, yours and theirs.

Sheep are woolly, you can't afford to be. Neither can you risk being boring. Boring is seriously bad. The style, the warmth and the hookability factor of your writing, says a whole lot about you, your approach to your business and indeed how your client relationships might pan out. In addition, people are always interested in finding out about the person or people behind the business, so you need to look carefully at the ins, outs, do's, don'ts and maybes of writing about yourself. Your aim should be to provide something that will grab the reader's attention, hold their interest and not have them glazing over before they've hit your second sentence.

Make Yourself Real

You want to write about yourself in a way that will make people read and remember. One of the ways you can choose to do that is by being unexpected, reaching out to seize attention, holding on to it with both hands and not letting go. Below, are a couple of different suggestions for the first parts of a biography to go on the About page of a graphic designer's web site. Both pieces of text are accurate, and there's nothing wrong with either. But because Option 2 is unexpected and off-kilter, it might hit harder and faster and paint a stronger personality and picture.

- **Option 1:**

I was born in Belgium, but I came back to England with my family when I was six. We lived in Northwood, Middlesex, because my father worked at the military base there. In school, I always enjoyed drawing and design and when I went on to university I took my degree in graphic design. I opened a graphic design agency in . . .

- **Option 2:**

I was extremely sick on a rough ferry journey when I was six years old and we were travelling to England from Belgium, which is where I was born. This has no relevance whatsoever to what I do now, but I never got the sympathy I felt I deserved at the time, and it's always rankled! Anyway, nowadays I own and run a graphic design agency which I set up . . .

This sort of quirky approach might or might not be for you, you might like it, you might loathe it and there's no definitive right or wrong as to whether you should or shouldn't. Choices like this are very personal - think of it like shopping for clothes, some outfits suit you, others you'll try on, yell 'yuk' and fling out of the changing-room immediately. Writing for your business is all about your decisions, your choices, your preferences. It's about feeling comfortable in your own skin and with the image you're projecting - but sometimes it's good to think about doing things differently, coming at it from an unexpected angle, surprising people.

Breathing in Short Pants

Yes indeed, I am now going to talk about contractions, but before you lunge for the gas and air, these are the ones you read or hear all the time, without them registering. I've been using contractions in my writing from the beginning of the book, it's simply the tiny difference between saying I've been using and I have been using.

If I drop the contractions as I carry on with what I am saying now, you will see the tone of the writing is immediately slightly different, you may not consciously notice it, but eliminating contractions changes both the tone and pace of the text. It will not change the sense of what you are reading, but it will subtly alter how you perceive it. It alters the flow, diminishes the warmth, makes it less conversational, informal and friendly and hence and most importantly, impacts on the connection between writer and reader.

Take a look at another couple of examples. This time for the About page of a lady who runs a nanny sourcing agency. Again, two versions conveying basically the same information, but with what feels like a completely different personality behind each.

- **Option 1:**

It was the birth of my own twins, together with problems I encountered trying to find and book a nanny, that made me decide to open my own business. I had previously worked as an administrator for a large distribution company and my organisational skills and logistics experience have helped enormously with the setting up and efficient running of the agency. My business partner brought to the company her own extensive experience as a nanny and we have now been successfully running Nannies to Go for over five years.

- **Option 2:**

When we went for the scan and the radiographer said, 'twins', my husband leapt to his feet, banged his leg on the trolley I was on, bent to rub it and gashed his head on the metal edge. There was blood everywhere and we ended up in A&E. So, I'm waiting for them to stitch him up and I'm in and out of the loo, maybe nerves, maybe shock, probably the gallons of water they make you drink before a scan. And I thought, I'm going to have to work from home when the babies arrive – but I'll need help. And then one of those two-birds-with-one-stone brainwaves hit me and, that's the moment I decided to set up Nannies to Go . . .

The second version is undoubtedly quirkier and therefore probably more memorable. It uses contractions and humour which makes it warmer and more immediate. Option 1 takes a more formal approach. Neither is right, neither is wrong, it's simply a question of preferences, choices and the sort of writing style you feel comfortably fits you, your personality and your business or profession. But I hope that maybe it gives you an idea of how the same facts can be presented so differently, and the scope you have for playing around with a range of options.

Sometimes you need to make a change to make a statement.

Chapter Five: Blowing Your Own Trumpet

"He who whispers down a well

About the goods he has to sell,

Will never make as many dollars

As he who climbs a tree and hollers!"

Whilst there's no doubt about the importance of the person and personality behind the business there's also no disputing that for many of us, blowing our own trumpet isn't an easy undertaking. Unfortunately, writing about yourself and doing it well is something that has to be tackled head on. The quote above sums it up rather neatly, there's no point in being in business unless you're prepared to shout about it, and part of that shouting has to be about you.

I'm going to stick my neck out here and make a gross generalisation – feel free to nod in agreement or yell in denial – but I'd suggest it's more often women in business who might have a problem with trumpet blowing. Think about how most of us deal with a compliment. Someone might say 'I love that dress'. What's the most likely response? Is it, 'Thank you so much, I love it too'. Or, might it be more along the lines of 'Goodness, years old, sale at M&S I think'. Sound familiar? A compliment given and deflected rather than accepted graciously. Nothing dramatic or earth-shattering, it's the sort of exchange you might hear and not think twice about - but what's actually going on? Is it that we hear other women doing it, so we're simply trotting along a well-trodden path? Does it reflect a concern as to how we'll be perceived? Is it simply a lingering lesson from childhood – 'Don't show off dear'.

No cut and dried answer, but it goes on often enough to make it worth thinking about how it impacts on the way women write about themselves, as opposed to how men might handle the same issue. When you're writing with the specific purpose of moving your business forward, you need to know your own strengths. If you don't recognise those, you're not putting your best foot forward. And, as a logical follow-on, if you can't realistically assess your own value, how in heaven's name are you going to accurately set charges for your services?

If this muted trumpet problem is something that's ringing bells with you (gotta love a mixed metaphor), can you change your pattern of behaviour? I think you can. I'm not proposing for one moment, when someone says something nice, you turn soppy and simpery, I'm simply suggesting you introduce a pause button. Allow yourself a second or two to assess what's been said, think about it and before dishing out that automatic disclaimer, accept the compliment. A small adjustment to programmed behaviour might have a happy knock-on effect when thinking and writing about yourself, your qualifications and your talents. False modesty is a luxury none of us can afford.

A Brief Thought on Emojis

Emojis have their place in communication, but my opinion – and you may completely disagree – is that care should be taken deciding where that place is and it's not necessarily in general business communications.

I realise I may be treading on a lot of toes here, but if you've written something amusing which needs to be underlined with an emoji, then perhaps it wasn't amusing enough! Harsh? Possibly. But worth thinking about because, unlike a communication going to a friend or colleague who know you well, anything that goes on your site, in your emails or anywhere else might be seen by a lot of people who don't. Emojis can convey all sorts of things, but is it possible the one thing they don't shout is professionalism?

Never submit a piece of writing without taking time to look at it in the cold light of day.

Chapter Six: Decisions, Indecisions & Directions

Are you an 'I' or a 'We'?

It's probably unnecessary to say - although we tend to forget what's right under our noses - when you're writing, you should always bear in mind where and under what different circumstances it's going to be read. Who are you addressing and what might their expectations be? You could quite comfortably opt for a quirky approach for your own website or a flyer, but would probably go for more straightforward and formal for a Linked In profile or an application to the Institute of Directors! That doesn't mean you're using a changed voice or that it's any less authentic, it just means there's a difference in choice and use of language.

Horses for Courses

What works a treat for one audience might not work as successfully, or at all, for another. If someone reading the text on your site is a potential client heading for a divorce and a worrying financial settlement, he or she won't want to be bowled over by a solicitor with a way-out sense of humour. On the other hand, a mother-to-be, looking to take on a nanny, might well be tickled pink to find the owner of the agency is someone warm and funny, with whom she can instantly and clearly identify. When you have a clear idea of who you're talking to, you have an equally clear idea of what you should be saying and how you should be saying it.

Who Do You Want to Be?

We or *I* is always a bit of a thorny subject and something many of us have to think carefully about, and even then, we might not come up with a satisfactory answer.

Obviously if you're in a partnership, practice or even just a two-person company, there's no problem, you'll use *we* when talking about the business. If on the other hand you're running a business or practice on your own, there's always a dilemma, with no definitive answer other than what feels most comfortable for you. You don't necessarily want to come across as too small, but it's pointless to try and make out you're heading up a vast organisation, if you're not. It's something that needs consideration and consistency, otherwise you'll constantly be getting your *we's* muddled with your *I's* and everybody, including you, will be dazed and confused.

Any decision is particularly pertinent when setting out a biography for your website. But there are always ways round this. For example, if on your site you've been talking about *we* throughout, a neat way to continue that, without misleading anybody in any way, is not having an *About* page, but perhaps a *Behind the Business* page. This allows you to put up your bio, as being the brains behind the business, and doesn't need to specify whether you're working with others or on your own. It also leaves the way comfortably open to add team members or associates as your business grows.

The next decision is, should your bio be in the first person or should it be in third? Would you prefer to talk about yourself or would you find it easier to make it one degree removed, as if someone else is summarising. Final choice rests purely on your own preferences, whatever you think sounds best for you and your business and what slips in smoothly with all your other text.

Nobody Likes a Smart-Arse!

If you're writing in the first person, you should probably be a little wary you don't sound too pleased with yourself, as you reel off your qualifications and expertise, whereas writing in the third person makes it easier to blow your trumpet just as hard but possibly more comfortably.

Below are a couple of examples over which you can mull. One is a biography for an Educational Facilitator and the other is for a Specialist Skin Therapist. Each of these are written out twice, once in the first person and then in the third. Have a read through to see the slightly different impressions they'd create if they appeared on your website.

- **Option 1:**

  First Person: Educational Facilitator

  I'm a highly qualified and experienced Trainer, Facilitator, Therapist and Consultant with senior-level psychology and counselling skills, along with executive-level business logistics expertise. I'm an excellent communicator. Bringing my skills to my work within NHS and charity sector, I've have found my interpersonal and organisational abilities have allowed me to facilitate smooth implementation of initiatives.

  I also run a busy private practice from my office in Surbiton, with a specific focus on children and teenagers, resolving the issues that can arise within families.

- **Option 2:**

  Third Person: Educational Facilitator

  Serena Morris is a highly qualified and experienced Trainer, Facilitator, Therapist and Consultant with senior-level psychology and counselling skills, alongside executive-level business logistics expertise. She's an instinctive communicator with an eagle eye for detail and an intuitive ear for nuance. Serena brings a unique skill-set to her well-regarded work within the NHS and charity sector. Her organisational abilities have led to her excellent reputation for smooth, comfortable and non-confrontational implementation of innovative systems and initiatives, with quantifiable financial and staff benefits.

Serena also runs a well-regarded private practice, based in Surbiton, where she works with children, teenagers and adults, helping resolve the many issues that can impact on family life and well-being.

- **Option 1:**

  First Person: Specialist Skin Therapist

I specialise in treating all types of skin conditions, as well as offering a range of beauty treatments. My clients say nobody spoils them like I do, and I'm flattered that people travel from all over the UK and abroad for my individually designed treatments.

On a visit to my studio you're made to feel instantly comfortable with warm and genuine hospitality, refreshments of your choice, and space and time to talk. My intention is to wrap you in a cushion of relaxation, ensuring you're de-stressed, nurtured and pampered in an atmosphere of calm tranquillity, to restore equilibrium and serenity.

I'm fully qualified in Aromatherapy and Reflexology, NLP, EFT and Life Coaching as well as in bereavement and counselling skills. So, whether you prefer to relax in silent contemplation or talk in completely confidential surroundings, you'll know there's always a listening ear to go with the magic hands.

I have lectured for the last ten years at local colleges, and am a sought-after trainer of advanced techniques for newly qualified members of my profession.

- **Option 2:**

Third Person: Specialist Skin Therapist

Roz Allen did her training over an intense three years in London, where standards were exceptionally high, and students were expected to work, work harder and then work harder still! She's been making people look and feel their best, ever since.

Whilst building her successful practice, and not being one to sit on her thumbs, Roz trained and qualified in additional therapies, including Aromatherapy, Reflexology, NLP and EFT, any of which may be incorporated in her bespoke treatments and facials, depending on the needs of each client. Roz is also a qualified counsellor and believes her listening skills are as important as everything else she does.

Roz's down to earth approach, genuine empathy and quiet humour, instantly puts people at ease and it's probably these qualities, as much as her skilled treatments and magic hands, that bring clients back time and again to relax in the tranquillity, calm and comfort of her studio. She's lectured, for the last ten years at local colleges, and is a sought-after trainer of advanced techniques for newly qualified members of her profession.

The above biographies of two different professionals show the amount of flexibility there is, in how you present yourself and although the information is more or less the same, there is a difference between it being written in the first or third person. Not better or worse, just different. When you're putting together your own material, it's what feels most comfortable for you, and which way of writing feels more authentic.

If you're not clear who you are and what you do, why on earth would anyone else be?

Chapter Seven: A Rose By Any Other Name

'. . . would smell as sweet'. Or would it?'

Let's imagine, way back, it was decided to call a rose a slod. Doesn't quite work the same way at all does it? Exquisite, delicate, scented, luscious, romantic – a slod? Please!

And here's another thought. Would we feel quite the same about Romeo if he was Fred? Would Juliet have stirred our emotions so deeply if she was an Ethel? And if not, why not? Is it just usage and cultural associations or is it that some words are simply more pleasing than others to our ear? Is a name simply something we get used to, or are there other factors at work? We all know, naming children can be a scary undertaking, but I'd suggest naming or re-branding your business is even more nerve-wracking. Your kids may hate you for what you call them, but if you get it wrong with your business, that's a far more expensive mistake.

When you're naming a business, what you're working with is not just cultural programming and expectation but also visualisation, comprehension and possibly the most important factor of all – common sense.

One of the things that can and often does happen is choosing a name that has deep or sentimental meaning for you. But the fact is, whilst it might resonate with you and your nearest and dearest, bring a smile to your face and a nice warm fuzzy feeling every time you hear it - it might be doing nothing at all for anybody else. If it's leaving them none the wiser as to who you are and what you do, then it's not the best choice.

Another hole into which you can fall, and you'd be surprised how many people do, is choosing a name which people aren't quite sure how to pronounce. This is not a good idea, if they don't know how to pronounce it properly, they're not going to be in any hurry to pass it along for fear of getting it wrong and looking silly. Of course, for every rule, there's an exception and you might at this point be raising a hand to point out that Seat Cars haven't exactly sunk without trace and this I cannot deny, but I'm still sticking to my general principle!

Working with Olivia

When selecting a name for your business or re-branding an existing one, there are two roads you can go down. Let's look at an osteopathic practice run by a young lady called Olivia Lang. Olivia has decided to go for a straightforward approach and call her practice by her name, nothing wrong with that. However, she does then need to tell people what she does, so she's possibly looking at her business name being:

OLIVIA LANG:

Osteopath

Straightforward, no fuss, does exactly what it says on the tin. However, is she missing an opportunity? If she made a simple shift and put her business definition alongside her own name, she'd then leave herself free to add a strapline, and if you've any doubt about how important a strapline can be, think about the phrase I just used. That Ronseal line, '*does exactly what it says on the tin*' is probably better known than the product itself. It's become a well-used and immediately comprehensible part of everyday language, and if that's not commercial success, then I don't know what is. Olivia could go for

OLIVIA LANG, OSTEOPATH

Your Path to Pain-Free

Or perhaps,

OLIVIA LANG, OSTEOPATH

We'll treat you better!

Or even,

OLIVIA LANG, OSTEOPATH

We've got your back!

Simply by adding a strapline, you immediately feel you know more about Olivia and her business than you did before. With just those two lines she's given you her name, what she does and a taste of the personality and brand of the business. Is your own name and strapline doing that for you? If not, it may be worth a re-think.

Write or Wrong?

As you know, laying down the law isn't what this book is all about, but when it comes to naming your business, it's so important you make the most of a name, a definition and a strapline, because they're all ways of raising your profile, and that's never to be sneezed at. You'll also have the confidence of knowing that nobody's ever going to look at your business card or any other material you put out and find themselves confounded, confused and clueless.

In the long run though, whatever advice you get, you can only be guided by your own gut feeling and - a brief word of warning here - however much it helps to gather the input of family and friends, never forget, people love being asked for their opinion, but ask half a dozen of them and you'll usually get eight different views. That isn't to say they may not be making good and valid points, but those points can often be diametrically opposed, providing you not with the answer you wanted but instead with a pounding headache and an urgent need to lie down somewhere quiet and dark for a couple of years.

Any kind of advice or input, from wherever it comes, is always best when sieved through your own common sense, like flour, it will always come out finer for the filtering. In the long run, having faith in and following your own gut instinct, will usually prove the safest way to go.

Parcelling it all Up

When information is passed from one person to other people, it needs to be packaged, and the smaller and neater the parcel, the easier it is to hand on to all and sundry. You want to hand out a package, not a problem.

What you want to tell people should be concise, correct, precise, and interesting. If it is, there's far more chance of it going into their head and staying there, as opposed to going in one ear and promptly sliding out the other. If you're not confident you're doing that and doing it well, you have a problem that needs resolving.

Think of your information as orange squash, the more water you add, the more diluted it gets. Words are similar, the more you add to them, the less strength they have. People don't remember long and complicated, especially since we've all adjusted to assimilating facts swiftly and succinctly from the web. The fact is, if we don't get what we want quickly enough, we don't usually pause to puzzle it out, we move on, we're spoilt for choice.

If your business card doesn't tell people what you do, then it isn't really a business card, is it?

Chapter Eight: Don't Murder Your Message

Keep calm and clarify.

Is your business message clear, or as clear as mud? Not sure? Well, on a scale of 1 – 10, how confident are you of the following:

- When you tell someone, or indeed a group of someones what you do, are they easily and immediately able to grasp what you're offering? Do you see in their eyes instant comprehension or more of a glazing over?

- Have you made it so straightforward for them to understand, they'll have no problem whatsoever passing it along to others?

Is Your Message Doing the Business?

If on those couple of questions, you're coming in at a 10, stop reading immediately and go and do something more interesting, you don't need any help. Anything less than a 10 and you, like most of us, could probably do with a bit of message massaging. But don't fling yourself across your keyboard in deep despair just yet, stand tall, read on, there are always solutions.

What we want from writing is clarity and, like so many other things, that usually boils down to common sense, plain and simple. Your message needs to be clean, lean, brief and unambiguous. And you should examine it from all angles to make sure that's the case, because that's how it will be looked at by potential clients and customers, who will all come to it with different agendas.

To be effective, successful and ultimately profitable, your business message needs to instantly tell people what you do or offer. At the same time, it needs to make absolutely clear why you're the best person to come to for that service or product. Not too complicated, but you and I know, there are any number of issues which can rear their ugly heads and put themselves in the way of getting that communication right and tight.

Clarity or Calamity?

There is no denying most of us suffer from more than a touch of verbal diarrhoea, it's a common affliction and made ten times worse if you're off-kilter. Maybe you've pitched up at a networking meeting you weren't sure you really wanted to attend, had to park miles away, gallop to get there on time and once inside, can't see a single familiar face. Such a sequence of events can either lead to you lurking uneasily behind a potted plant for the duration or buttonholing someone, anyone, and talking way too much.

Talking too much is always a risk, particularly because most of us share the unshakeable conviction that the one thing we don't mention, when telling someone about our business, will be the very thing they wanted to know and that alone will be enough to lose that potential client.

This is the reason, whether we're writing or talking, that most of us veer in the far-too-much direction, thus diluting our message completely. When you're writing, you have the chance to go back and edit ruthlessly, usually to the benefit of the text, sadly that doesn't work if you're verbally babbling.

It's therefore worth working on the structure of your message by writing it down, turning it around, twisting it inside out and playing with it until it's down to just a few sentences. Learn and use them. In effect you have a script and you'll be surprised, not only at how much better that makes you feel, but how much more impressive it makes you sound.

Let's imagine your business is catering, you're introduced to someone at a networking meeting and they ask you what you do. You might say:

"I run Deliciously Different, we're caterers, we do business conferences and events, birthdays, weddings and funerals too. Oh, and family parties, we do a lot of those and retirement dos. We also run cookery classes in schools for children. And we have regular courses for adults at our premises - it's a great way to meet people with similar interests. We cover Beds, Bucks, Herts and of course, central London too. Cakes, I forgot to mention our fabulous cakes, in fact we just won a national award for one of our wedding ones!"

Now, whilst all that information is accurate, you've just hit someone with a heck of a lot of it. Which bits will stick? Which won't? Have you totally watered down your core message? In fact, what is your core message? What aspect of your business do you most want to promote?

Are you a business that goes into schools as an outside resource, to run cookery classes? Is that your main source of income and therefore what you need to push first and foremost?

Alternatively, are you running a cookery school, but you also provide event catering?

Or maybe your main business is the event catering, with the cookery lessons just a side-line?

On the other hand, do you want to focus on and grow your award-winning cakes operation?

Your business is wide-ranging and encompasses all the above - and good for you, you're using your specialist skills, staff and expertise to diversify and grow in interesting and potentially profitable directions. But, by taking a step back and deciding which aspect you want to be perceived as core and which as supplementary, you immediately make your message less confusing. What should also then become clearer is who exactly you're talking to.

- Is it people within schools, who make curriculum decisions and also have influence on out of school activities?

- Is it adults who want to further their knowledge by attending cookery courses and meeting others with similar interests?

- Is it individuals or companies who are or will be looking for catering services?

- Is it people who are in the market for your speciality cakes – the wedding market for example?

I know, a lorry-load of questions, but pulling a business, any business, apart in this way, allows you to analyse, understand and prioritise. However, the only person who can do that is the person who's launching or running it, because none of the options above is necessarily better than the others, it's purely dependent on the direction in which the business owner wants to take it.

Let's, for the moment, assume in this example that your main money-earner is the catering service and the other sections are supplementary. You want to develop and grow them in time, but right now, it's the catering that's bringing in the money.

This might then lead you to think about altering your name. **Deliciously Different** doesn't actually tell people what you do, does it? With a simple change to **Deliciously Different Catering**, you could immediately knock that issue on the head.

And, as your business name now defines you more clearly, you could use an additional strap line in either of two ways. You could choose an aspirational statement to convey the spirit of your brand, or you could offer further clarification on the different areas of your business. These are the sort of suggestions I might make:

DELICIOUSLY DIFFERENT CATERING

Food that Tastes as Gorgeous as It Looks

DELICIOUSLY DIFFERENT CATERING

Exceptional Food for Your Event

DELICIOUSLY DIFFERENT CATERING

Exceptional Food for Your Exceptional Event

Or,

DELICIOUSLY DIFFERENT CATERING

Event Catering ~ Award-Winning Cakes ~ Cookery Courses

DELICIOUSLY DIFFERENT CATERING

Event Catering & Cookery Courses

DELICIOUSLY DIFFERENT CATERING

Award-winning Event Catering & Cookery Courses

All or any of the above, could work well for you, and simply having your name and strapline neater, tighter and doing a better job, allows you to re-look at your message script which you might now find easier to wrap in a neater package. Don't panic if you're not mentioning absolutely everything in that package, better to give an overview than an over-cluttered one. You could therefore comfortably say, in answer to the *What do you do?* question, something like:

"I run Deliciously Different Catering, gorgeous food for every type of event. Our food's as good as it looks, and our cakes win awards. We also run cookery classes in schools, and for adults at our own premises."

The advantage of keeping your wording brief means, whilst you might not have covered absolutely everything, you've summarised enough to interest rather than confuse and it's succinct enough for them to take in. I should point out, I'm not suggesting you stand to attention and reel your script off robot-fashion, nor is it a good idea to have it written on your hand in case you forget, but it doesn't hurt to have it in your head, so you can bring it out appropriately.

When it comes to all the other phrases and ideas you've put together, nothing's wasted – you now have a bank of different copy lines. Choose the one you want to use consistently with your business name and utilise the others elsewhere. For example, you might have a business card something like this:

DELICIOUSLY DIFFERENT CATERING

Food that Tastes as Gorgeous as It Looks

Marian Pemberton

Director

www.dddcatering.co.uk - talk@dddcatering.co.uk
0208 000 0000 - 00000 000 000

Event Catering ~ Award-Winning Cakes ~ Cookery Courses

London, Beds, Bucks, Herts.

Having worked through the evolution of the business message above, you'll see how you can apply it to your own business and you'll find, to your surprise, if you ask yourself the right common-sense questions, you'll usually come up with the right answers. You'll also see, when you have your message and summary clear and comfortable, how the rest of your marketing material text - website content, brochures, meeting presentations – flows smoothly, because it's based on a firm foundation.

A waffle's for breakfast, not for a business message.

Chapter Nine: Marketing Hits & Myths

If you're running a business, you're marketing, if you're not marketing, then you're not running a business.

Of all the words bandied about, and goodness me, a lot of bandying does go on, *marketing* is probably one of the most misunderstood, misused and generally devalued. If that sounds a little harsh, forgive me, but over the years I've seen more unproductive money poured into that particular pit, than I've had hot dinners. The fact that in the early days of my business career, some of it was mine, doesn't make me any more mellow!

Don't misunderstand, I'm not casting aspersions on the many sound, sensible, professional and proactive experts out there who specialise in marketing your business. They know what they're doing, and they do it well. I'm merely pointing out that until *you* have a completely firm grasp of what you want marketing to mean to you and for you, you're almost certainly not going to be able to lay your hands on the right people to help, in the ways which will be most effective.

You Can't Afford to Gamble

Nobody wants to throw their money around willy nilly, yet so many of us unintentionally and foolishly do. Because that's what happens if you go ahead with something you haven't first clarified in your own mind. I know, I know, I've said it before, but as you'll have picked up on by now, that's not going to stop me saying it again.

Unless what you want is clear in your head, you don't have a hope in hell of getting it clear in anyone else's. It's as essential to convey what you want to say to those professionals whose input you're seeking, as it is to get it right for your prospective clients and customers. If you fall short on the first, you're going to fail miserably on the second.

Selling Yourself

I recently came across a definition of marketing which went something like this: ***Marketing is the management process responsible for identifying, anticipating and satisfying customer requirements profitably.*** Well, you can't take issue with that, it's not wrong. Personally, I'd prefer to put it more simply, I'd say: ***Marketing's a state of mind.*** Why? Well, if you had to jot down a list of things that *didn't* come under the heading of marketing. What might you list? Possibly not a whole lot because marketing, in its broadest sense, takes in every channel and method you might use to get yourself under the right noses. It includes such essentials as:

- Naming.
- Branding.
- Business cards.
- Brochures, flyers, catalogues.
- Website.
- Social media.

- Newsletters.

- Press releases.

- Signs and posters.

- Advertising & advertorials.

- Networking.

- Blogs.

- Sales letters.

- Workshops, talks and presentations.

- Telemarketing.

- Media exposure.

- Trade shows.

- Word of mouth.

All the above, rest on the strength and standard of your branding and under branding, as well as consistency of colours, graphics and design you'd probably also want to include other basics such as:

- The way you treat/communicate with your clients, your employees, your suppliers.

- The way you dress when you turn up for a meeting and whether you turn up on time.

- Whether you let your mobile interrupt your meeting.

- Whether you're prompt at returning emails, and if you don't have an answer someone needs, letting them know that and reassuring them, they'll have the information as soon as you do.

- How you sign your emails.

- How your phone is answered and how promptly calls are returned.

- How and when your invoices are sent out, whether they look good, whether they're carefully checked for accuracy and how you deal with chasing them up if they're not paid.

None of this is rocket science and I'm not telling you anything you don't already know, although sometimes, when we know something, we tend not to give it a lot of thought, and not thinking can lead you down some money-wasting one-way streets and dead-end roads.

Communication's King (or Queen)

You can see how important the strength of communication is, in action and appearance as well as writing and speaking. If you're not doing and saying the right things, the right way, to the right people, you won't do well. It doesn't matter whether your product or service is the best in the world and it makes no difference if your marketing budget runs into millions or is so slim that if it turned sideways you wouldn't see it, clear communication verbal and non-verbal is key.

If there's one place we don't want to see our money go, it's down the drain, so none of us can afford not to market and market well. This means it can be short-sighted, to put things in different boxes and try to run them individually. Every aspect of your business is intrinsic to all the others (think intermeshing cogs). The bottom line is; if your service or product isn't reaching and being bought in increasing numbers by clients, if it's not making more money than you're spending, then what you're running isn't a business, it's a hobby, and an expensive, stressful one at that.

Procrastination Never Makes Perfect

If you accept marketing and communication are as entwined as Romeo and Juliet (although hopefully with a happier outcome), and that those two elements encompass every part of your business, the upside is you're always looking at the bigger picture. By looking at that bigger picture you'll avoid many problems that so many businesses, large or small, established or newly-launched encounter, because they're looking only at separate segments and not the whole - I think a Chocolate Orange is a great visual for this, but that might just be me.

I'm sorry to say though, that an acceptance of this whole picture theory, does rather knock the wind out of the sails of the procrastinators amongst us who might be content to murmur, 'I'm waiting to do some marketing until; my website's ready; my brochures are printed; I've got new stock in; I've taken on a new member of staff; I've given some thought as to how I want to approach it.' Truth is, you can't afford to let the grass grow under your feet, not unless you're prepared for a lot of weeds to sprout up too.

When the going gets tough, the tough market more.

Chapter Ten: Help Wanted

Don't get disconcerted, discombobulated or desperate.

There's an overwhelming amount of information and input out there, whispering seductive promises of business success in your ear. But what with being busy looking both into the future and focusing on the now, squinting at the bigger picture and getting that flipping message to make sense, it's not always easy to find time to consider what might work well for you, as opposed to what won't and indeed, who you should be listening to as opposed to ignoring.

Goodness knows, there's advice, inspiration, books and workshops galore from any number of professionals, each of whom is an expert in their own field, although sometimes those fields can overlap in confusing and contradictory ways. There are wise and weighty statements from industry gurus and mind-blowingly triumphant stories of others doing what you do, yet apparently doing it startlingly more profitably. It can be tough to make the right choices for you and your business, but whilst I'm all in favour of getting in expert help, before you make decisions, or even enquiries, make sure you've thoroughly thought through what you need. I've put down some of the practical points worth considering.

Market Appropriately

There's little benefit in spending pots of cash on a marketing campaign, however brilliantly conceived, executed and successful, if you can't service it. Little point in having clients falling out of the woodwork, if you haven't got the time to deliver the products or services you've promised. Instead, you'll find yourself running around like a blue-bottomed fly, and at the end of the day you'll be disappointing, letting down and losing customers whose attention you've just paid a lot of money to capture.

The above may make so much sense that it's not worth wasting your time saying it and honestly, I wouldn't, if I hadn't seen it happen time and again. There's no denying a great marketing campaign is one that brings in a big response, but success can't be measured by response, only by the successful fulfilment of that response.

If that seems logical to you, it'll also ring true that before you approach anybody whose professional skills you might need, you should know what it is you want from them, the extent of what you want and that when it comes to budget, you're both on the same page. Some or all of these details may and probably will change as things move forward, evolve and grow organically. But at the starting point, remember, waffling takes and wastes time - yours and theirs. So, do everyone a favour and work on the waffle before, not during a meeting.

Filling in the Gaps

There are no hard and fast rules about who you should and shouldn't get to help you launch, re-launch or grow your business, but there's no doubt that at some stage you will need help, because there are only a certain number of things you can do on your own. And even if there are things you don't mind 'having a go at', you need to calculate whether it will cost you more time and frustration than it would if you got someone else to do it. You'll know where your strengths lie and equally, where your shortcomings may be lurking.

If you're not good with figures, find someone who is. They'll be able to whizz through the stuff that gives you a headache, because that's their job. They can look, tell you where you're going right, where you're going wrong, whether you need to make changes and how to make them. Once you've done that, you'll know you're proceeding in the right direction rather than running around in ever decreasing and possibly unprofitable circles. We all have things we love or loathe doing and that's no failing. Some of us are great on day-to-day stuff, others are grand at planning ahead. Some are brilliant at implementing things with drop dead efficiency and logistical skills, whilst others are choc-a-bloc full of ideas, just a bit vague and disorganised when it comes to putting any of them into action.

Take a long, hard look at what you're good at and what you enjoy (usually those two go hand in hand), and then fill in the gaps. If you're rotten at paperwork, find a good Personal or Virtual Assistant who's never met a mess they couldn't sort. If you loathe cold calling, find someone who doesn't have such an emotional stake in doing it and won't sink sobbing to the floor, if hit with an unfavourable response.

If you're a solicitor launching your own employment law practice, odds are you may not be particularly design-orientated. If you're a graphic designer, setting up your own studio and taking on a couple of staff, you may not be a dab hand at knowing how to put together an employment contract. As a skilled nutritionist, you may be brilliant at sorting out digestive systems, but completely in the dark as to how to reach potential clients. As a gifted teacher, moving from tutoring privately to establishing a private tutorial school and taking on staff, you may be über-fluent in German, Spanish and French, but unable to speak a word of bookkeeping! I could go on, but you're way ahead of me by now. First you need to identify the gaps that need filling then find the people to fill them.

If you have a well-thought-out requirements list, both you and the person you're approaching will know what exactly you're after. You may want to get a few quotes and have meetings with two or three different experts, but you'll be handing them the same set of requirements, so you will be able to judge what they say and what sort of fees they're going to charge, on a like for like basis. If you don't have that concise and clear spec, you can't get a concise and clear quote and this can lead to grief further down the line.

The other important factor, and never underestimate this, is finding someone on the same wave-length as you. If someone sets your teeth on edge when you first meet them, odds are they'll have you grinding them as you move down the road with any project. Trust your instincts, if you don't feel someone is the right person to work with, then they're probably not.

Creative Flow

You may know exactly what it is you want to write and, as we've discussed, could probably do it yourself, but if you feel there's a risk it will take more time, blood, sweat and tears than you're willing to waste, find someone for whom getting information onto page or screen is a walk in the park. If it's a professional who earns their living doing this, it's to be hoped they'll be good at what they do, and it can take a weight of worry off your shoulders.

But, however good they are, they won't be telepathic, so you do have to let them know what you want your clients to know. They should then be able to step into your shoes, and not only convey your message, but also the brand and personality of your business. If you're clear, your writer can be clear too and if you're not yet clear, then a professional should be able to help you get your thoughts and message in order.

My advice, before launching on a writing venture with anyone, is get them to do you a short sample piece first. It need only be a brief paragraph or two, perhaps a re-write of some marketing material you already have, but you'll be able to tell if you like it and if you feel they've 'got you'. Any copywriter will be more than happy to do this, after all, in the long run it saves them a lot of angst too.

Cash Flow

Sometimes it can feel cash flow is flowing in only one direction, and it's not the right one. Budgets, large, small or non-existent, play a vital part in all and any business decisions. But there are often imaginative ways of handling cash-strapped situations. You might find experts in their field, are equally desperately looking for experts in yours and a barter deal can be on the table.

A disingenuous question that's sometimes asked when receiving a quote can be 'Is that your best price?'. This is really not a sensible query, why on earth would someone waste their time and yours giving you anything else other than the best price for a service? What's really being said is 'I don't want to pay that amount; will you bring it down?' I don't feel this is a great way to start a working relationship and in reality, can prove disadvantageous to both parties. The service provider if they want and need the work may be forced down on the fee, but is not thrilled. The client, achieving a revised price might have concerns as to whether they're going to get what they paid for!

My suggestion would be, rather than haggle, if you're concerned at having to pay a chunk of money at the end of the project – and that's a legitimate concern - ask whether staggered payments would be acceptable. In many cases, they are. By approaching it this way, you won't have forced a discount, but you will have both a smoother cash flow and a more harmonious relationship.

Additionally, you can always as they say, 'think out of the box'. You'd be surprised how often people are open to new ideas, innovative thinking and expertise exchange that gives both parties what they want without too much money changing hands. But you can't afford to be coy, ask the questions you want to ask and the worst that can happen is you're given the cold shoulder, in which case you know that's not a shoulder to be leaned upon. When it comes to what you can afford to spend on any particular service, put your budget on the table, ask how far that will get you and if it gets you nowhere with that particular expert, then carry on looking for another one.

Prioritise, cherry-pick, match-make.

Chapter Eleven: In And Out Of The Elevator

If you don't make yourself interesting, people don't remember you.

Most of us in business do some form of networking, and if you're not doing it then you should be, it's probably the most effective way of getting your business under other people's noses. It also provides you with an incredible resource of professional support, service providers and chances to form beneficial, strategic business alliances you might never otherwise stumble across.

As an added bonus, and who doesn't love one of those, it also makes you supremely popular with friends and family. They know they can always ring you for the name of an expert in any given area, however obscure, and you'll be able to lay your hands on one straight away, and on the odd occasion you can't, you'll be able to make a phone call to someone who can.

Networking works well, because colleagues get to know and (hopefully) like you and use your services. Of course, as with anything else, it's important to put in the effort and you have to be sure you're giving people the information you want them to have.

Always be aware though, word of mouth is an incredibly powerful tool but, like a chain-saw, use it clumsily and things won't turn out so well. Going the extra mile for clients pays off, selling them short doesn't, and negative comment spreads as far and probably faster than anything else - it's a risk never worth taking.

Stand and Deliver

Most structured and regular networking meetings give everybody the chance to talk about their business – usually one minute for what's called the elevator pitch - and just because the time you have is limited, doesn't mean you can't achieve what you're there for. After all, you're not doing this just for kicks, you're paying an annual subscription and probably paying for a breakfast or a lunch too. Are you capitalising that outlay? Because doing a minute's presentation is more than just telling people about your business, it's giving them a chance to listen to you, take to you and remember you.

What's Your Approach?

Everyone approaches a networking meeting slightly differently – and I'm not making judgements here, having at one time or another certainly done all the things I'm busy recommending others not to do.

Some people, the *Well-prepareds,* are passionate about getting their minute written and under their belt, at least a week or two before it's needed. Then there are the *Last minuters,* cheerfully certain fate will step in and present them with divine inspiration as they rise to their feet and open their mouths. Unfortunately, divine inspiration sometimes takes a day off, which means both they, and everyone else, is fully aware there's a fair old bit of unprepared waffling going on. Also, it's tough to judge your timing when you've no idea what you're going to say, so you invariably haven't got to where you think you should, before a timer goes off and everyone expects you to sit down.

Done and dusteds, on the other hand, whilst smugly reassuring themselves they've got this, can fall into an entirely different trap. They'll pitch up, clutching their slightly crumpled, carefully written minute, knowing it's gone down very nicely at the last five meetings and should be good for at least another few. What they overlook is that when people hear the same thing over and over, they may remain politely smiling and apparently attentive, but they've probably switched off and are trying to recall whether or not they took the chicken out of the freezer before they left the house that morning. Thus, whatever it is you're saying may well be sailing over heads like so many helium balloons. Or maybe you're in the *I'll be fine* camp? This conviction often only lasts until you're actually in the meeting, at which point you panic and decide you might not be quite so fine after all. You'll then be that person desperately trying to scribble unobtrusively so nobody will notice, although of course they will, and they'll know exactly what you're doing, because we've all been there at some time and done exactly that!

Gazing or Glazing?

The writing of your minute is far too important to leave to either chance or habit. Given that those 60 seconds of business promotion are as valuable as they are, doesn't it make sense to be as sure as you can that you're holding your audience? Because, an audience isn't always an easy thing to hold.

If, for example, you've been a member of a networking group for any amount of time, when you stand up to speak, people will already know what you do and there lies the rub, they may think they don't need you. Your aim, where possible is to demonstrate they couldn't be more wrong. Let's just assume for the moment you're an Independent Financial Adviser, you're going to be addressing a group of people with different agendas and you have a wide range of services to offer them but:

- There may be those who could do with financial input but are nervous of looking at things too closely. *Can you reassure them talking to you needn't be a terrifying experience and their figures might not be half as worrying as they fear?*

- There will be individuals who've used a financial planner in the past and not been that impressed. *Are you able to show you're a very different type of personality?*

- There will be people who have no clear idea of the scope and range of what you can offer. *Can you make them aware of that?*

A lot of issues there, but that's probably not an unreasonable assessment of the different ways, individuals round the table at that meeting might be thinking. Each of us needs to define for ourselves what approach is best to pull in clients or customers, no matter what business or service we provide. Is there a perfect formula? I wish there was, in which case I'd be a far richer woman than I am. But I'm not pulling the wool over your eyes and I don't have a wand to wave, there is no magic solution. I can however offer some practical suggestions and foundations on which to build, which you may or may not find helpful.

Gotta Love a List!

It's an irrefutable fact that life's hectic for most of us, but why we so often pile on extra stress by leaving things to the very last minute, is one of those great unanswered questions. At risk of sounding slightly pious (heaven forbid) I'd point out that while some events come upon us unexpected like, others are totally known about in advance. There's nothing you can do about the unanticipated, which tends to hit you on the back of the head like a plank of wood, but you can deal with the anticipated, such as the minutes you're going to need for networking. And whilst you're dealing with them, it makes sense to wrap them up for around six months or so, think of the peace of mind that might give you.

Below is the sort of thing I might suggest to our Financial Planner. I haven't written out the complete content of each minute, but by putting together a list like this, she'll have the confidence of knowing in advance exactly what she's going to do each month. It will do away with any last-minute panic, not to mention the complete absence of inspiration that always hits you when time's short.

By setting things out this way, she'll be able to see she's covering subjects that will catch the attention of a variety of people with various issues, at different times. It also means her listeners won't ever know quite what she's going to say or do. She won't bore them and by utilising a bit of the unpredictable (who'd expect an IFA in a clown's hat?) she'll hold their attention. She'll be building up a strong personality and her visual props will stick in people's minds. She'll be doing everything she possibly can to make an impact and she won't be easy to forget.

SIX-MONTH MINUTE PLANNER FOR OUR IFA

January

- **Prop** - *Paper Bag.*

As you stand to speak, pull a large paper bag over your head for the first sentence. You might have to speak louder to be heard and please note – paper bag, not a plastic one, otherwise things could go horribly wrong.

- **Theme/Content**

"Is This You When It Comes to Financial Planning? *(Remove bag and continue). Just because you're not looking at them, doesn't mean issues aren't there. You might find looking at them is easier than you thought. Ditch the paper bag, you'll be surprised how relaxed and relieved you'll feel."*

<u>February</u>

- **Prop** - *Piece of Rope.*

Dangle a short length of rope or thick piece of string from one hand.

- **Theme/Content**

"What's this? (pause) It's a life-line. (pause) and it couldn't be more important to you and your family when you most need it. Life or critical illness insurance and pension planning are essentials. Reach out and grab the lifeline – you won't regret it."

<u>March</u>

- **Prop** - *Blindfold.*

Slip on an eye-mask (cheap ones obtainable from Amazon.)

- **Theme/Content**

*"**This is a blindfold.** You wouldn't wear one to run a marathon, why would you wear one to run your financial affairs? Follow this up with appropriate questions:*

~ Pension plan?

~ Power of Attorney?

~ Will?

~ Savings?"

April

- **Prop** - *Clown's Hat.*

From fancy dress shop or Amazon. Put on hat as you stand up.

- **Theme/Content**

*"**Nobody expects Financial Planning to be a laugh a minute.** But once you've got it sorted, you'll feel a lot more like smiling."*

May

- **Prop** - *Stethoscope (Real one would be great, but don't mug your GP - a toy one will do).*

- **Theme/Content**

"When was your last financial health check? You get your eyes tested, you go to the dentist, you have the car MOT'd. Who's keeping a finger on your financial pulse?"

June

- **Prop -** *Cuddly Toy Cat or Cat Photo.*

- **Theme/Content**

"Are you a Scaredy Cat? Worried you don't understand financial planning but scared to ask? Don't be, If you've got questions, I've got answers. Let's have a no-charge, no commitment chat."

Keeping an audience on its toes means no-one's dozing.

Chapter Twelve: Action Plan

Steer clear of anything that might get up people's noses or on their wick.

We're probably all agreed, it helps, when you stand up to present your minute, if people don't instantly take against you, but when it comes to your communication and presentation skills, how you say what you're saying, is as important as everything else. A few suggestions:

- Always look up and make eye contact with people round the table while you're talking, this makes everyone feel included, keeps their attention and stops them doodling pretty patterns in their notebook.

- It's important to speak slowly and clearly and a beat - a pause in your presentation - is as important as everything else. You'll often see a beat instruction in scripts, because pausing at the right time, in the right place gives people a chance to absorb what you've said or to chuckle, without then missing your next words.

- When it comes to your minute, less is more. You don't want to rush as if you've a train to catch and although lots of people time themselves beforehand, that's not always the best way to judge, because it doesn't allow for reaction time from an audience. You're possibly better off to plan your minute to a word count. You can feasibly fit in nearly 200 words in sixty seconds, but only at a mile a minute gabble. Ideally, around 170 words is comfortable, it allows you time to pause and look up, as well as breathe - always helpful.

- It's not a great idea to run over your minute. Once a timing device has gone off, you're going to lose people's attention. They're distracted by the sound and embarrassed that you don't appear to have heard or are ignoring it. So, whilst you might be able to slip in a couple of dozen extra words, they're probably falling on deaf ears and it doesn't make you look professional.

- Whilst you're speaking, it's a good idea to move a little, turning the angle of your body slightly as you talk. In this way, you'll be making sure you address all sections of the group. But keep the movement minimal, you want to avoid looking rigid and unrelaxed, you don't want to look as if you've got ants in your underwear.

We all have little habits or tics of which we're blissfully unaware, and were we to have them pointed out, would no doubt be mortified. But we're all grown-ups here, and a little mortification never hurt anyone, so I'll come right out and say it. Could you possibly be a hair-fiddler; a nose-stroker; a necklace-twister; a glasses-taker-offer; an earring-adjuster or a compulsive bra-strap-retriever?

None are earth-shatteringly dreadful and in the short time you're standing, they're probably not going to over-irritate your audience. But harmless little habits give out messages that may not be accurate. They can make people think you're nervous, that you lack confidence in your profession, product or service. These assumptions may be miles from the truth, but if that's the impression you're giving, then you're undermining your carefully thought through minute.

Finally, the most important thing you can do is smile. If you smile, it's likely your audience will smile too, because as human beings we're programmed to mimic others even if we don't realise we're doing it. Thus, whether you gave your minute perfectly or cocked it up completely, at least everyone will look cheerful.

Feel like a ramble?
Then grab a rucksack and head into the woods, not into a meeting.

Chapter Thirteen: The Wonders of Websites

Creating a website can feel like getting a demand from HMRC, you know it's got to be dealt with, but you're far from thrilled.

If you're in business, you need an online presence. In days gone by you wouldn't have run a business without a phone on which you could be contacted, it would have made you look a little daft and a lot shifty. The same nowadays applies to your online presence. It may or may not be the primary way people find you, but whether they Google and you come up, whether they take your business card and follow up or whether they get a personal referral from someone and then check your site - it's vital you look and sound as good as you want them to know you are.

Bells and Whistles – Old Hat!

Nothing in life or business stands still, and technology rushes forward faster than anything else, which means our expectations are constantly changing. Websites, their design, functionality and the way we write for them have evolved too. There was a time when bells, whistles and devilishly clever visual gimmicks left us gobsmacked, deeply impressed and riveted to the screen as they unfolded in all their glory, such a site was the sure sign of a successful, cutting-edge business.

That's not the case anymore - think of your own requirements when you want to make a purchase or get information. What're your priorities? Do you want to take the time to waft in a leisurely fashion through an artistic introduction, or do you want what you're after as quickly and simply as possible?

Functionality is as important as form – perhaps more so now than ever before. Presentation and professionalism are, of course, still vitally important, but websites are like any one of us - there's no point in looking great if you don't work very well.

Bust Those Barriers

We're unanimous on the importance of good communication and clean, clear writing. What is interesting though, are the artificial (usually unconscious) barriers that can be put up, between the way we talk and act when face to face, as opposed to how we write about our products, services and indeed ourselves.

Most of us are reasonably endowed with common sense, but when it comes to writing for your business you may find your confidence in that, slipping silently down the plughole. Which, when you reflect on it, is odd. After all, you're not generally struck speechless when introduced to someone in a business context. You're perfectly capable of adjusting the way you talk, the words you choose and the way you use them. You do it without thinking and most of the time you manage perfectly well.

Think about what you do when you meet, or are introduced to someone in a business context. You know you need to smile, because if you stare at them expressionlessly they'll feel uncomfortable, they'll be even more alarmed if you frown. And most of us know, without thinking, just the right level of smile - not too little, that can feel chilly, not too much, that can be scary (think about clowns). And it probably goes without saying, you'd stick to a smile, laughing out loud would put the wind right up them, wouldn't it?

We utilise touch too, when we shake hands and most of us, with a few exceptions (President Trump?), know the right strength and length of that hand-shake. Too long and too tight isn't great, it's a domination thing. Too short and not tight enough, results in a dead-fish-feel and that's not encouraging either.

One of you is likely to make a small joke – in Britain, the traffic, or better still, the weather's always a safe bet. We don't think twice about any of these familiar rituals, we just perform them. We use them to oil the wheels of communication, to break the ice, to get a feeling of who we're talking to and once we've followed the prescribed steps, we can then move comfortably on to business.

When we write, we use our words to duplicate all the things mentioned, and if you think about it that way, it can make it much easier to express what you want. You'll find if you ditch some of your concerns, learn to lean more heavily on things that already come naturally to you and rely on common sense, it'll usually see you right. Just a few small, simple adjustments to your thinking, will allow you to use the power of words to mimic the communication tools you're already so well used to wielding.

I Suppose You Think That's Funny?

One of the issues that comes up time and again, when talking to people about business writing, is the use of humour. There's a strong perception (fear?) that whilst humour and warmth can be embraced in the spoken word, when it comes to writing, there's a risk it will diminish professionalism. As a result, there yawns a gaping chasm into which charming, clever, witty and naturally bubbly people drop their personality, before putting together the wording for their websites or brochures - they're trying to fit in when they should be trying to stand out.

If you are a naturally warm and funny person, isn't your personality and warmth the very thing that makes you and your business different from others and attracts the right sort of client? Don't don a mask that isn't you, it doesn't pay in the long run.

Bottoms on Seats

If you have doubts about the power of humour, think about speakers you've listened to over the years. The difference between a good one and one who makes you want to slide gently off your chair and rest on the floor until they've finished, is usually down to the warmth and humour of their personality.

A speaker who's a natural (or lucky enough to have a canny speech writer) will usually start their talk with something that makes everyone chuckle, it doesn't have to be a rolling-in-the-aisles joke, just something to draw people together. It means that what started off as a group of individuals, changes subtly but instantly into something completely different - a tribe for a brief while. Anything else that follows, then falls on far more receptive and accepting ears.

A Time and a Place

Humour can be the greatest leveller, door-opener and easer of atmospheres, but as with all interaction, it operates within its own parameters. When it's right, we're quick to appreciate it, but are swiftly made uncomfortable by the unexpected, inappropriate or bizarre, so it's important to get it right.

A young, buzzy, innovative branding agency can afford to have a website that's a bit on the wild and wacky side, whilst a financial planning partnership specialising in inheritance tax, wouldn't be aiming to have people falling off their chairs laughing fit to bust!

But even that's not as cut and dried as it might sound. Our branding agency can't afford to get too carried away with wild and wacky, they need to be certain that potential clients are also fully supplied with all the practical, professionally laid out business information they need, to make them want to pursue things further. By the same token, our financial planners certainly don't want to project dry and dusty, so their writing needs to be leavened with one or two lighter comments to establish empathy with clients, who will want to see them as warm and approachable, as opposed to intimidatingly formal and unapproachable.

Striking the right note is important and some people are instinctive communicators, the ones who know, without thinking, what will work and what won't. But if you stop and think about those you know, who fall into that category, you'll realise a large part of their charm is their ability to make you laugh, to enjoy the time you spend with them. The aim therefore is to make your website warm, welcoming, informative and inclusive. It should make people feel they're listening to a person they've taken to, and that person is talking directly to them.

Underestimating humour as a communication tool
is a mistake you can't afford to make.

Chapter Fourteen: Wondering About Your Website?

If everyone isn't singing from the same song sheet, you'll get headaches, not harmony.

Your main aim when looking for the best professionals to work with, to move your business forward, is to have everyone singing from the same song sheet. Many years of experience have taught me, this isn't always as easy as it sounds. Therefore, because I'm a simple soul and like life to be as stress free as I can possibly make it, I've fallen into the habit of using an information/Content List.

This is particularly useful when putting together content you might want to include on your site. By setting up a list, you can play around with ideas, switch things around and see exactly what you're doing. At the planning stages, you might find this sort of list invaluable as you get your bafflingly tangled thoughts in order, and it can make website planning more of a doddle than an ordeal.

Perfect Packaging

Once you have your content listed, you'll know what you want on your site, you'll then know what to write or, if you're working with a copywriter, what you want written for you. Once they've completed that to your satisfaction, you'll have both the content and text to take to a web designer.

Your web designer will be beyond delighted to get their hands on such a detailed, neatly packaged plan and can then get to work placing that content in a smoothly-functioning, good-looking site. You'll be saving yourself and the people you work with time, money and recriminations being exchanged at any stage, because everyone can see exactly what they're working with.

Below is an example of a general information/Content List. You can see at a glance what's there, what's not, what should be, what might be discarded or what needs adding to aid clarification. You can also see how easily it can be adapted, with different page headings to suit the specific needs of your business or practice.

WEBSITE INITIAL CONTENTS LIST

- **Home Page**

  Overview so the business is instantly identifiable.

- **Products & Services**

  Overview of what's on offer, perhaps with *'read more'* click-throughs.

- **Product or Services Details**

  You may or may not want to include fees or prices in this section.

- **Way We Think/Work**

  This might or might not be a section you'd want to include.

- **About**

  Biographies of who's behind the business.

- **Testimonials**

  You might have a page of these or choose to place them throughout the site.

- **Contact**

  Contact info, plus other any other practical stuff such as location, hours of business, parking etc.

- **Gallery**

  For any business with shots to display.

- **Shop**

  Shop and shopping cart if selling online.

- **Blogs**

  Blogs, plus industry relevant news and articles.

COMMENT ON CONTENT LIST

Home Page

On the first page of your site that people see, you're aiming to replicate the communication you'd use if meeting someone in person. Warm, friendly, professional and efficient, giving them the information they need, without wasting their time. The sort of thing going through the mind of the reader is likely to be:

- What is the business?

- Is it what I'm looking for?

- Does it sound like a company I'd like to use?

- Can I see clearly where to click next, to find out more?

Products or Services

If you have a broad base of products or services, you can always offer a menu with a brief line of introduction/explanation and a 'read more' click-through option. This means that rather than having to wade through a load of information, the reader can immediately focus on the specific item or services in which they're interested. After all, if they were face to face with you, that's what they'd do, they'd ask what they wanted to know, and you'd tell them. You can do the same on the site in a straightforward, instantly understandable way.

Further Details of Products or Services

Here you might want to consider whether you plan to include your fee structure or prices. Always a difficult decision and one on which everybody has a different view. Some people would say where there's no indication at all of cost, it's like wandering into a shop of gorgeous but unpriced shoes – you have no idea whether you can risk looking around and falling in love, or need to back out, sharpish.

Others would say, putting fees on your site might put people off, although I wonder then if you need to re-look at them to make sure they're appropriately placed in your market. A happy compromise can be using 'from'. By putting 'From £ . . .' you're giving people an idea of whether they're in the right place, but at the same time giving yourself leeway for your prices changing or adapting to different clients and circumstances.

The Way We Think/Work

This might or might not be something you'd want to include, depending who you are, what you're doing and whether you feel it's relevant. You might consider it helpful to offer information on different methods or practices within the business. For example, if you're a therapist who provides different treatments, you might want to talk about the background of those treatments and why you've chosen to qualify in those.

This section might also apply if you're a professional such as an accountant or solicitor. You'll probably have a wide range of services available, and pride yourself on a particular approach to client relationships, which you would want to include.

About

This would be about you and whoever else is behind the business. You may also want to include additional, shorter biographies of other individuals, if you work with a team. This page can be highly effective, because it rounds out the personality of the company perfectly and if you use head shots, people can put faces to names.

It should also be noted that whether your professional background is relevant or not to your current business, it can be hugely powerful in unexpected, if not necessarily logical ways. For example, an alternative therapy practice can benefit enormously if the therapist has a background in conventional medicine or science. Including this fact, might well bring in clients who are on the fence when considering alternative treatments, but will be reassured by seeing you've come to it from what they'd consider a conventional route.

Testimonials

You and your designer will discuss how client testimonials can best be displayed. You may decide to have them all together on one page of the site, or place them on different pages. Whatever you decide though, never underestimate the strength of testimonials and client feedback. These are even more powerful when a website or contact details of the testimonial-giver are included, giving potential clients the confidence of knowing they can check if they choose to. They rarely do, but confidence is often more about perception than reality isn't it?

Contact

Your contact information is obviously essential, and you should give details of your location. If you're running a business from a home office, you may not want to put your address on the site, but you can give the area and then a detailed address once you're in contact with the client.

Parking or travel details are also helpful, as are hours of business and an idea of the range of appointment times available should someone be specifically looking for an evening or weekend.

Gallery

A gallery is a wonderful way of displaying a variety of shots and there are any number of businesses who would benefit from this - photographers; interior designers; artists; specialist cake designers or hat hire companies.

Shop/Shopping Cart

Your web designer will have all the expertise to advise on the best purchasing and payment systems to set up. But you're the expert on what you're selling, so you need to present all the information such as professional product shots, clear, succinct item descriptions and of course, prices if people are buying online.

Blogs

To blog or not to blog, that's the question and if you do, then you should include the blog on your site. There's no doubt, blogging can raise your profile substantially and these written pieces give insight into you, your views and how you run your business. But, if you're going to blog you need to do it regularly.

T & C's

Every business should have a set of Terms and Conditions and this applies whether it's just you, plugging away on your own from the kitchen table, or whether your enterprise is a far larger affair altogether.

Official Stuff

Your website designer will of course advise you on all the legally required privacy notices you should include on your site, which I won't even venture to go into – as far as

I'm concerned, cookies are things that come with nuts and chocolate chips.

Final Word on Websites

There are any number of companies that can offer you templates, so you can build your own website, rather than using a professional web designer. There's no doubt this is going to be cheaper in the short term. However, only you know your own capabilities or limitations when it comes to this sort of thing and, as always, it's a question of carefully weighing up what's going to cause you the least grief and aggravation.

Don't try fitting in, when you should be trying to stand out.

Chapter Fifteen: Down And Dirty

Some writers swear by systems, others just swear.

There's no set way of working on your writing, and I wouldn't dream of telling you there is. There are people who swear by systems, working to a formula and always in a specific order. My view is that every writer, whether of fiction or business texts, has their own individual approach, and who's to say what's right or wrong, as long as the end-result satisfies requirements and is understood by the reader it's designed to reach and appeal to.

If I show you the way I might work through a project with a client, you can follow my train of thought (although this comes with no guarantee I won't go off the rails). You might then, if it makes sense to you, use the same sort of thought process as a jumping-off board, whether you're planning to do your own writing for your business, or get some outside help.

Setting up a Beauty Business

Let's talk about an entrepreneur called Florence. She's just signed a lease for a high street shop and is launching a Beauty Salon. The salon will provide all the usual services, alongside a range of aesthetic treatments from relevantly qualified specialists working on a freelance basis. Florence has been the manager of a Knightsbridge salon for a number of years, but has her own clear idea of the ways in which she wants her own business to be different.

The premises she's taking on are on the high street of a small town and carry heavy overheads, but she's done her figures and is confident these can be met. She also plans to increase her revenue by renting out the four fully equipped private treatment rooms, when they're not in use by her own staff. She plans to rent to practitioners looking for part-time premises. The rooms would be ideal for people such as aromatherapists, nutritionists, hypnotherapists, acupuncturists, etc and Florence has already established there is a demand for practice space in the area. The benefit to her would not only be rental revenue, but an increased footfall through the salon. In turn, the individual therapists could benefit from being part of a multi-disciplinary centre, where all sorts of issues from beauty to well-being can be accessed.

As a qualified and accredited trainer, Florence is also able to offer apprenticeships and Continuing Professional Development courses to therapists working in the beauty field. This provides yet another revenue stream.

Over her years in the business, our Flo's also naturally had a great deal of experience working with various cosmetics and skin care products and has opted to use three specific, high-performing Italian brands in the salon. Because these aren't obtainable in the UK, she feels there's an opportunity to sell them in-store and online too.

Why, you may wonder, am I setting this up for you in such detail? It's because I think it demonstrates how, by working logically and systematically, even a business that appears complicated, can be presented clearly, pulling together that all-important message, getting the brand image right, and at the same time, covering all the facets that need to be covered.

Name and Strapline

By the time we sit down for our first meeting, Florence has done her share of agonising over a business name. She originally compiled a long list of possibilities, then nearly gave herself a nervous breakdown by consulting family and friends, each of whom had a different, albeit equally strong opinion. She's sensibly chosen to ignore most of these and go with the name she originally wanted.

The name she's chosen is Orchid Aesthetics which is good, symbolising elegance and beauty, at the same time as being a strong visual – when people can picture something, they tend to remember it more readily. I wonder though, whether there might be a risk using the term aesthetics on its own? Might it slant perception of the business too much towards the aesthetics side and away from the more traditional beauty treatments on offer? I think that's worth thinking over and playing around with some options whilst keeping the visual orchid element. I think an added strap line is important, in that way, we can widen the field to take in beauty and pampering as well as the more technical aesthetic treatments.

My first step is to put together a selection of ideas for her to work with because often, only by comparing options, can you become clearer on preferences. It will be Florence's choice as to which name and strapline she goes for, but by reviewing and weighing up pros and cons, she has the chance to see how she might more clearly define what's on offer.

Mix and Matchable

As you'll see, many of the straplines suggested below, are interchangeable and could work well with more than one of the names, so there's a fair amount of choice. I generally recommend not using the same word in the name as in the strapline, for example *beauty*, but it's not a hard and fast rule. I am however a great believer in never throwing anything away, so once a specific strapline has been selected to appear with the company name, the other straplines can be pulled into service for other purposes as they all describe and enhance the brand. They can be used at the base of web pages or would come in handy for future marketing, you're setting yourself up with a *text bank* of useable phrases.

Looking Good

The input of a graphic designer, when you're creating the name and logo that's going to be the face of your business is, I believe, essential. Most of us, unless trained, aren't graphically knowledgeable, but having said that, the difference between a home-grown name and logo and a professionally designed one is immediately and glaringly obvious, even if, like me, you couldn't name a font if it came and bit you on the bottom. The fact is, if your logo and name don't look professionally slick, your business doesn't look professionally slick. I know cash flow is always tight, but failing to ensure your logo, name and strapline look as good as they can, is an economy that will do you no favours at all.

Name and Strapline Suggestions for Florence:

THE ORCHID SALON

Treat yourself Beautiful

ORCHID AESTHETICS

The Beautiful Body and Face Place

ORCHID AESTHETICS

Lending Nature a Helping Hand

ORCHID BEAUTY & AESTHETIC TREATMENTS

Looking Good!

ORCHID BEAUTY & AESTHETIC TREATMENTS

Perfect Pampering

THE ORCHID

Aesthetics & Beauty Treatments

ORCHID AESTHETICS & BEAUTY TREATMENTS

Pamper yourself Properly

ORCHID AESTHETICS & BEAUTY SALON

Bare-faced chic!

ORCHID AESTHETICS

Face and Body Beauty

ORCHID SALON

Bring out the Beautiful

Website Information

After some discussion, Florence decides on Orchid Beauty & Aesthetic Treatments for her name and Treat Yourself Beautiful for her strap line. The next step is to help her get her thoughts in order, by setting out all the different strands of her business plan in the form of content for her website.

A Content List is invaluable when it comes to telling your web designer what you want, but it's also helpful for

Florence, because it takes all those ideas and plans chasing their tails in her head, and lays them out so it's far easier to see what's what. It also means, that as I work with her on the text, we're both singing from that same old song sheet I've talked about before. Both of us can see what's in there, what isn't, what should be added, what might be taken away and possibly whether the order in which we're giving the information should be switched around to make it more logical and understandable.

The example below is the first incarnation of the Content List and is complete enough for Florence to take it to one or more web designers. Obviously, once a talented designer gets their creative hands on the list, the page order and all sorts of other things may change and be placed elsewhere, but at this point, they have what they need to know about what Florence wants included. They'll be able to give a realistic quote and if she's getting quotes from more than one designer, Florence will be able to compare them, like for like, so she can make the best choice.

ORCHID BEAUTY & AESTHETIC TREATMENTS

Suggested Information Content List

- **Home**

Overall view of the business & how it makes clients feel.

~ Sign up for our newsletter and regular special offers.

~ Current offers available.

~ Salon news; awards; press coverage etc.

~T&Cs

Privacy Details, Cookies etc.

Our Treatments

Drop-down menu with choice of click-through to either **Beauty** or **Aesthetics**

Beauty Treatment & Price Guide

~ Manicure.

~ Pedicure.

~ Brow & Lash Tinting.

~ Facials.

~ Spray Tan.

~ Skin-care consultation & treatment etc. (Florence to add further details as relevant).

Aesthetics Procedures & Price Guide

~ Laser hair removal.

~ Semi-permanent make-up.

~ Micro-dermabrasion.

~ Injectables etc. (Florence to add further details as relevant).

- **About Us**

  ~ **Florence's** biography & head shot.

  ~ **Introducing Our Specialist team:**

  Details of individuals, their specialisms, qualifications, experience + head shots.

- **Shop**

  ~ The brands we use and our reasons for selecting them.

  ~ Product details/ shots and shopping cart.

  ~ Product feedback from clients.

- **Contact Us**

  ~ Full contact details.

  ~ Salon address & location map.

  ~ Opening Hours.

  ~ Parking.

  ~ Local transport.

  ~ Client Testimonials.

- **Therapist Career Opportunities**

  ~ **Therapy Rooms for hire:**

  ~ Therapy Rooms: details of rooms and equipment.

  ~ Therapy Rooms: Terms.

  ~ Therapy Rooms: Booking.

~ **Accredited Professional Training Courses for Beauty Therapists:**

~ Dates.

~ Duration & cost of workshops/courses.

~ **Apprenticeships**

~ Details of Apprenticeships.

Having sorted the information Content List into a logical order which covers everything that Florence wants to include, the next stage would be to write the text for each section. In this way, along with the Content List the web designer then gets a full text for each section which can be placed appropriately in the website design which has been created.

The whole thing should run like clockwork, although we all know that life and business being what they are, spanners on occasion can be thrown into the works and cause hitches, hold-ups and hysterics. Despite this, I still feel you can't beat getting your business structure and thoughts down in an orderly fashion, and if things do go a bit haywire at any time, just make yourself a strong coffee and cuddle your list - in the long run it won't let you down.

The more information you give to your web designer, the more they're going to love you and the better job they'll be able to do.

Chapter Sixteen: Standing In Florence's Shoes

If your business voice isn't right, the right clients won't hear it.

Florence is not only a canny businesswoman but also has a great sense of humour and firm ideas as to how she wants her new business to speak to clients. She's asked me to do the writing for her, so I need to be able to step into her shoes, use her 'voice' and convey what she wants clients and potential colleagues to know, both about her and about her company.

In her previous career, Florence managed a high-profile beauty salon which was part of a chain. Based in Knightsbridge, there was a regular clientele, but also a large stream of transient clients only in the country for a short while and usually directed to the salon by a hotel concierge. She is now going to be in an out-of-town, high street setting, which will present her with a completely different client demographic. She will want to build ongoing relationships with her customers, at the same time as standing out from local competitors. She feels that it's the whole beauty salon experience she's selling, and that the pleasure of that should stand alongside the excellence of the treatments. It's likely that the majority of her clients will be women and therefore her marketing will be directed at them.

She's seriously unimpressed with salon websites which plunge headlong into their range of treatments, because she thinks that's not nearly personal enough. On the other hand, she appreciates she can't have an introduction that's too wordy. Based on her thoughts, I've put together a suggestion for her home page, which hopefully ticks the right boxes.

Home Page. Text Suggestion

ORCHID BEAUTY & AESTHETIC TREATMENTS

Treat Yourself Beautiful

Life for all of us can be hectic, which is why, when you book in at The Orchid, you can expect an experience of pure leisurely pleasure. We think your enjoyment, is just as important as how good you look and feel when you leave us.

Our luxuriously soothing salon offers a warm welcome; supremely skilled therapists; uniquely sourced products and a complete range of treatments.

We can't promise you'll leave as a new woman, but we can guarantee you'll go out a whole lot happier and more relaxed than when you came in.

As you see, the intro is informal, conversational, includes a bit of humour but at the same time, promises highly professional treatment. It also makes it clear how important it is to the business that each client has a great experience. Below, is another text sample, this time introducing the section on semi- permanent make-up.

Semi-Permanent Make-Up Introduction. Text Suggestion

Let's face it, applying and removing make-up is a chore. Our semi-permanent make-up specialist offers you the chance to look great, from the moment you wake, till the moment you slide between the sheets again. You can relax, secure in the knowledge that you can hit the gym, run, swim, shower or weep buckets at a wedding, all without getting that distinctive panda-who's-been-out-on-the-town look.

We've used the same conversational, talking to a friend tone to introduce the procedure and convey the important selling points. This can then be followed by detailed information on choices available, prices and an idea of how long it takes, lasts etc.

Lined up and Ready to Go

Florence now has her project (and her mind) more in order, and because she knows exactly what she wants, there's going to be a lot less wear and tear on the nerves of all working with her, a lot less room for misunderstandings, misinterpretations or wasted time. The web designer is now in possession of:

- The information Content List.

- A document with the completed text written out for each section of the site.

- Treatment listings with full information and prices.

- Biographies and head shots.

- Product details and prices.

- Contact and location information.

- T & C's including appointment cancellation policies.

- Details of treatment rooms for rent.

- Details of apprenticeships and professional training opportunities.

Additionally, should Florence decide to bring in a marketing, PR or social media specialist to help her spread the word, she has all the information to hand, for them to work from too.

There should be three C's on every website - clarity, coherence & consistency.

Chapter Seventeen: Killer Copy Lines

Killer copy lines are great, but only if they work. Simple and straightforward is often more effective than subtle and sophisticated.

There's no doubt copy can sometimes be far too clever for its own good, and a line is only as great as the reaction it provokes. It's only successful if it does what it's supposed to do, and does it for the maximum number of people who read it.

We've all seen marketing campaigns, which undoubtedly came across as brilliant, when presented by an over-excited ad agency, but subsequently fell flat on their face. It's one thing, when you're in a room with a group of like-minded, creative individuals, all thinking along similar lines, but any copy that's obscure, can die a slow death once it heads off and reaches real life consumers. And marketing material that doesn't hit the spot it was supposed to hit, isn't successful marketing. Not only is a miss as good as a mile, but it translates into a lot of £s, which might just as well have been flushed down the toilet.

So, is there a magic formula for getting your writing right? Dear readers who've stuck loyally with me this far, I'd love to say yes, but there isn't. If there was, I'd be sipping Piña Colada on a beach somewhere and counting my money. However, despair not, we can aim for the next best thing which is, in my experience, a certain amount of instinct, a lively imagination and a lorry-load of common sense.

Playing Around Pays Off

You have a huge amount of scope when it comes to playing around with names for a new business or a re-branding, and there's always more than one, indeed often several that will work equally successfully. I'd suggest that most of the brow-furrowing and head-banging that tends to beset people at this stage, can be eliminated. All you need to do is successfully communicate what the business *is* and ***does***, and that's it – job done. If we take another couple of examples, you'll see what I mean and how the process might apply to your own business.

Francesca Leoni runs a planning and building-projects business. This includes organising and managing internal reconfiguring, conservatories and loft extensions as well as an interior design and supply service.

She's been in business for ten years but has never really branded properly, just used her own name and done a great deal of explaining as to the extent and range of what she offers. She wants to rectify that, present herself more professionally and bring in new clients, who will already understand from her information, what it is she can do for them. Below are some suggestions as to how she might go about this.

As you'll see, the first couple of options are practical in that they give the facts the client needs. The next four also say what the business does, but take things a bit further by adding something of the aspiration and intention of the brand.

Francesca Leoni Interior & Exterior Design

Complete Project Management

Francesca Leoni Design

Interior & Exterior Project Management from Conception to Completion

Francesca Leoni Interior & Exterior Design

Perfectionist Project Management

Francesca Leoni Interior & Exterior Design

Stress Less Project Management

Francesca Leoni Design Interiors & Exteriors

From Planning to Perfection

Francesca Leoni Interior & Exterior Design

Perfect Project Management

None of the above are right or wrong, you can see how they could all work. The final decision rests on personal preference. If you're doing your own name creating, the most important question to ask yourself is, 'If that wording is on a business card, is it crystal clear what the business is and does?' If the answer's no, or there's an element of uncertainty, then you're back to the drawing board.

Less Easily Defined

Naturally, some businesses are much more easily defined than others and if you're finding a precise definition is tricky, the answer can be to focus on the solutions and results you present as opposed to exactly how those are achieved.

Martin Addison is in his early fifties. His company produces beautifully crafted and styled educational toys for nurseries and schools and also supplies selected toy shops. The company has established its own niche market and whilst the toys are not cheap, they sell well because they're practically unbreakable, and last longer than less expensive options. Martin started back in the 90's as Sales Manager and when the business founder retired, he took over as MD. Since that time, he's taken the company to new levels and from an employee number of 15 to 300. He's now ready for a change.

He's always been as fascinated by people as by products and processes. He's seen the exponential difference the former can make to the latter two. He knows there are those who are natural and instinctive leaders and innovators, but believes such talent can always be enhanced and honed and techniques taught.

He has resigned from the toy company to launch his own executive level training business. His target market will be MDs, CEO's and business owners as well as financial institutions, government and non-profit organisations. He's going to be talking to those who appreciate how vital it is to nurture leadership talent to ensure continuity of success.

Martin has some concerns that he's entering an already crowded sector of the market. There are a lot of companies offering similar services and assurances, although as with all sectors of business, there are those who are highly effective and those who are not. But it's difficult to convince potential clients of your quality of service in advance, especially as the business won't establish its reputation for some time, nor will it have a portfolio of results.

My advice in this case would be that whilst the new company doesn't yet have a reputation, Martin does. I'd therefore suggest the focus of the name, brand and marketing should be based on the tangible successes of his previous career. The first four suggestions below feature his name, whereas the final two are more generic. If he decides he prefers to go for more generic naming, I'd suggest ensuring his name features prominently and early in any accompanying text. For example, I'd summarise in a brief line or two, his status and achievements, on the home page of his website.

Addison Executive Advancement Training
Leadership Evolution

Addison Advancement
Leadership Enhancement Training

Addison Advance Training Services
Good Leaders Communicate, Poor Communicators Don't Lead!

Addison Advancement Training
Because the Best Can Always Be Better

Addison Accelerated Leadership Training
Bringing Out the Strengths

Leadership Training & Development
Good Leaders Lead, Better Leaders Evolve

Leadership Training Evolution
Good Leaders Never Stop Learning

Any of these names give a reasonably clear indication of what he does, and further material would highlight his proven experience in taking a company to a completely different level. It also leads him along a logical path as to how to move forward. Whilst what he offers is applicable to any number of businesses and organisations, it makes sense that initial approaches should be within the toy and educational industries, where his name is known and doors are more likely to open for him.

We all have our share of common sense – trust yours.

Chapter Eighteen: Killer Copy Comment

You need to attract clients, but you need to attract the ones who will welcome what you offer.

Where the business is a sole enterprise and rests on the shoulders of an individual, the personality of that individual is key to the brand identity, vital to what the business offers and almost automatically selects who the business is talking to.

If the personality of the individual is unique and idiosyncratic and they have the courage of their convictions, there are all sorts of opportunities for creative marketing which can stand head and shoulders above the rest. Unconventional and challenging marketing can be an interesting and productive method of promotion. It also means you specifically attract clients on your wavelength rather than those who totally won't get you and what you're offering.

Sarah Calderson is a self-labelled trouble-shooter, trouble-maker and business analyst. She specialises in working with small to medium enterprises and, to quote *'Taking them by the scruff of the neck and shaking them into better business processes.'* She's loud, funny, never pulls her punches and doesn't hesitate to speak as she finds. She's also exceptionally well-qualified, has a high level of experience and expertise and an intuitive knack of getting straight to the heart of issues that may be holding a company back. She has produced some truly astonishing turnarounds, that speak for her abilities.

However, and she's first to admit it – she's not for everyone. She needs to attract the sort of client for whom she'll be a good fit, ones who can, as she puts it, *'Take it on the chin'*. She's previously been wary about coming on too strong, so when she originally launched, she kept her naming, branding and website similar to others in the same line of business. But bland and uniform simply isn't her, and she's now ready to take that on.

My thought is we could go against the grain - instead of selling her and her business to companies, why not challenge them, apply a sort of natural selection process. Clients who like the sound of her, will take it further, others who don't, will run as fast as they can in the opposite direction. It all comes down to setting expectations accurately. I put together a selection of names and straplines to see what might work. As you'll see, the first two are setting the right tone, whereas the others are a little tamer and more traditional.

The Calderson Analysis Programme

Kicking Your Business Up a Gear

Sarah Calderson, Change Specialist

Putting Your Business Firmly in Its Place

The Sarah Calderson Process

Turning Business Around

Sarah Calderson: Business Turnaround Consultant

Expertise, Inspiration, Implementation

Sarah Calderson Business Processes

Taking You to Where You Should Be

Sarah Calderson

Identifying Issues, Implementing Improvements

Sarah Calderson: Business Turnaround Specialist

Analysis & Implementation

Sarah Calderson

Business Analyst & Trouble-Shooter

The name and line Sarah opts for is:

Sarah Calderson, Change Specialist

Putting Your Business Firmly in Its Place

We now need to look at ideas for her new website which she wants to be different, not only from her original one but from anything else in the same field. She's ready to stand up and stand out!

The text for her homepage could read something like the example below. It doesn't hold back, the tone is challenging, but hopefully tempting to businesses who feel they're stuck in a rut. The challenging home page could be followed by details of her processes, qualifications, biography and several business case histories with testimonials. In this way, we're balancing her unconventional approach with her level of professionalism and quantifiable successes which speak for themselves.

Home Page. Text Suggestion

Sarah Calderson, Change Specialist

Putting Your Business Firmly in Its Place

Sarah Calderson cuts to the chase, eliminates the flim-flam, takes your business by the scruff of the neck and shakes it up every which way. She's known for challenging preconceptions, examining expectations, clarifying communication, defining direction, creating commitment and implementing improvements.

A recent client sums up his experience of working with Sarah; *'Exhausting? You bet. Successful? Not half!'* If you and your business are at the stage where you're ready to move on and up, call for a chat . . . .

You are your own unique selling point.

Chapter Nineteen: Stand Up, Stand Out

If your website text is indistinguishable from any other business in the same field, it needs some tweaking.

A lot of your new business will come from personal referral and word of mouth, people will then check out your website as an endorsement of that referral. On the other hand, if someone is Googling, they'll be presented with a heck of a lot of companies who do the same thing you do. The decision they make, as to whether to stop and read what you have to say, is made in a matter of seconds. If your site hasn't grabbed and gained their attention in those few seconds, you may well have lost a client.

Becky and Lisa are Software Troubleshooters, specialising in sorting out IT problems. They had their website designed and written when they launched, three years ago, it now feels a bit stale and what's more, sounds almost identical to others in the same business.

The girls are happy with their name and strapline which says clearly what they are and do and I agree – if it's not broken, why fix it? They're on a limited budget and despite wanting changes, can't afford for those to be major.

Their current home page text is straightforward and factual and there's nothing radically wrong with it, but I believe we can convey the same information whilst creating much more of a personality, with a headline and text to hook attention. Once that's been done, it would only need a tweak or two to text on subsequent pages to maintain the same slightly humorous tone, throughout. In this way, we can alter the whole feel of the business, at a minimal cost to them.

SOFTWARE TROUBLESHOOTERS

Rapid Response Service & Solutions

IF YOU FIND YOURSELF UP AN *IT* CREEK WITHOUT A PADDLE, DON'T THROW IN THE TOWEL!

We love nothing better than sorting out disasters, glitches, gremlins, break-downs, bugs, corrupted programmes and hysterical clients.

We have a passion for creative logic, alongside a somewhat obsessive-compulsive attention to detail. Nothing excites us quite so much as a seemingly unresolvable problem, although we're not just for blue-light emergencies. We also devise, build and support software applications to meet your specific business needs.

We maximise cutting-edge technology, optimise cost effectiveness, simplify operations and soothe a lot of fevered brows. So, should you find yourself up an IT creek, call us.

~

Jonathan Dixman, is a garden designer who's found himself up against the same problem of standing out. Like most other garden designers, on his website he's currently showing shots of gorgeous gardens he's designed and put in place. However, he knows the gardens displayed on competitor's sites, look pretty wonderful as well, what's going to make someone stop and choose one over the others?

My suggestion is to not show the beautiful results of Jonathan's work on his home page (he can put those up, further into the site) but to headline his home page with shots of pure delight - people laughing with pleasure, open-mouthed in surprise, hands to wide-eyed face, punching the air in excitement – you get the picture, and then the text we could use might be:

Jonathan Dixman

Designing Your Garden, Your Way

We could show you the gorgeous gardens we create, but we'd rather show you our clients' reactions. Because we don't just design perfect gardens, we design *your* perfect garden, the garden that's going to make you happiest.

We bring skill, imagination and specialist knowledge to every project and never come over hot and bothered, even when presented with the wildest area to be tamed and transformed into an oasis of tranquillity. You tell us what would make you happy - we make it happen.

In this way, not only does Jonathan's home page immediately look different from those of competitors, but he's putting his emphasis on the individual client. By using the visual impact of clients' emotions, he's sending out a strong message of what he's offering, which is as much about pleasure, as it is about the perfect garden.

Business writing is only ever as good as the amount of business it brings in.

Chapter Twenty: Expectations And Exasperations

When two people approach the same project, they usually come from opposite directions with different expectations.

None of us set out to waste time or money, yet isn't it odd how often we manage to do just that – and often in a quite spectacular way. Can this be avoided? Probably not completely, but there are some thoughts and suggestions I can put your way that might prevent a certain amount of hair-tearing and, trust me, I speak as someone who's learned the hard way.

Whether you're launching a new business, re-branding an existing one or simply focusing on keeping your company image visible, there are always decisions to be made, actions that need to be taken and new marketing material that must be produced. There are any number of excellent professionals who can help you with all of that, but the successful (or otherwise) relationship between you and the expert you turn to for help, needs to be based on mutual understanding and expectations. If this isn't the case, you're well on the way to hurtling down an extremely slippery slope and wasting a fair amount of that time and money we've been talking about.

Clarity Must Be Two-sided

Whatever type of creative process you're going through, the same rules of communication apply.

Whether you're working with a graphic designer; packaging designer; web builder; copywriter; branding expert; book formatter; printer; PR agency or indeed anyone else you might need to help you move your business forward, if you don't convey clearly what you want, then they're not going to know. If they don't convey clearly the extent of what they're going to do for you, then you're not going to know either.

Both parties may think they've communicated accurately, but I've seen enough misunderstandings, misinterpretations, disputes and despair arise in my time, to know you should heavily dot every *i*, firmly cross every *t*, never take anything for granted and preferably get things in writing. Problems rear their ugly heads when two people approach the same project with the best of intentions, but differing assumptions and expectations.

Avoiding Ugly Head Rearing

Let's assume for a moment you're a graphic designer who creates brands and builds websites. You've just had a meeting with a new client who's launching a Home Styling business. Her speciality is going into houses to improve their appearance, suggesting small changes and improvements to make them as attractive as possible, and thus easier to sell. She's already chosen a name and strapline for the business:

PRESENTATION MAGIC

Solutions to Speed your House Sale

She wants a logo designed as well as a logotype created for the name and strapline. This will be used on her cards, brochures, website and on future marketing material. She's exceptionally keen on using the *magic* as her theme and wants a wand with twinkling stars, incorporated in the design to illustrate this.

You have some reservations about whether this type of branding is ideal for her business which will be aimed at professionals - estate agents, landlords and developers - as much as individual house sellers. However, after talking this through, she's adamant this is what she wants. Following your meeting you send her a quote for creating her logo and then designing and building her website. She's happy with the quote and time-frame and you start to set up design ideas for her.

Your normal practise is to provide a range of options, so the client has a choice of designs for the logo with different colours, fonts and presentation. Having worked on these you send over a selection of four options for her consideration.

A week or so later, just as you're about to chase her, she comes back to say she's really sorry, but she actually doesn't like any of them and can you do some more? She still wants the *magic* theme and she's not exactly sure what it is about the current selection that she doesn't like, so she can't give you an indication of what she'd like to see done differently, she just knows none of them has really hit the spot for her.

That's OK, although you hope the client will like your initial suggestions, you know this isn't always the case, so you say you'll create another range of options for her which you do. This time she instantly loves one of the designs, says it's exactly what she had in mind and you're absolutely brilliant. She wants to go ahead immediately, which means as well as completing the artwork for the business cards and some flyers, you can also start work on the elements of the website. So far, so routine.

A week later, you submit the design for her site. You then get a phone call from her. She's had a radical re-think. She's concerned the *magic* theme might be too frivolous after all. She has decided on a new name and strap line for the business which she feels still has that special something, but is more professional. She now wants to call the business:

SHOW OFF

Interior Design & Property Presentation

Obviously, this calls for a new approach and new design, but you're a professional, you may do a little private tooth-grinding, but in the long run, the client is always right. If that's the direction in which she now wants to go, you oblige with a cheerful three-point-turn, and head off to do what she wants. You say you'll have some new designs for her within the next week. You also mention you will issue an interim invoice for the work done to date.

And This Is Where Things Can Turn Tricky

You've followed your client's instructions with two different ranges of design choices drawn up to her specification and instruction. She has subsequently changed her mind completely, which she's perfectly entitled to do. But effectively she's asking that you start the job again from scratch.

- **Your expectation** is you should charge a fee, for the time spent on the two lots of work you've already done, following her instructions.

- **Your client's expectation** is you haven't earned any fee, until she's 100% happy.

Unfortunately, like so many of life's little issues strewn in our path, there's no clear-cut answer as to how you deal with the above and I can't tell you how you should proceed, because there are always a multitude of other factors involved, not least of which is that you don't want to lose the client or the project. However, you feel it's reasonable that you should be paid for the work you've done to date, because whilst it's her privilege to change her mind, that's not your fault.

- **As the service provider:** you want to take as many practical steps as you can to avoid this sort of problem arising. Your terms of business should be unequivocally clear. Be specific about how many different design submissions are covered under the terms of your original quote. Make it clear, if further additional work is requested, above and beyond, this will incur additional charges. Most importantly, you need to make sure your client understands this from the off, and whilst I don't advocate getting anyone down on the floor with a knee in their chest, you should be firm about it. It's also helpful to put this in writing when you issue your quote.

- **As the client**: the more precise the instructions you give to the professional you're working with, the more accurate the result you're going to get. Of course, it's utterly frustrating if what you get back from the professional doesn't make you happy, but it's sometimes constructive to think the situation through from a completely point of view.

Imagine you wake up one day and decide you want to brighten your life and have your living room painted yellow. You call in a decorator who spends two days painting the room. When it's finished you take one look and hate it – far too overpowering, you've changed your mind, you now want the room repainted immediately, in good old reliable Magnolia. Another couple of days work. Under those circumstances the decorator would expect to be paid for his first couple of day's work as well as for the second two days, and it's my guess, it wouldn't occur to you to question that. After all, it wasn't his fault you changed your mind. It's no different when working with a creative professional who's designing or writing something for you.

Been There, Done That

In case you think I'm being smug (perish the thought), I should come right out and say the reason I'm pontificating at length about all of this is I've been there, done that, seen the subject from both sides and still come unstuck more times than I care to remember or talk about.

As a service provider, I understand all the reasons why, when you're starting a working relationship with a client, you don't immediately want to thrust before them all the things that might go wrong and cause you to fall out. It's rather like being in the first throes of a romance - it doesn't strike quite the right note to hammer home the importance of putting a pre-nup in place, for when all turns sour.

I don't think there's any sure-fire way of iron-cladding the thorny issue of   expectations at the start of a project and naturally, depending on what it is you do, there will be differences as to how you quantify your work and fees. If it will help, I can show you what I say to my clients when I issue a quote. Is it an infallible solution? Frankly my dears – I don't think anything ever is!

CREATE COMMUNICATION: TERMS & CONDITIONS

Relevant to project commencement:

- We have given a quote, based on our professional assessment of the time it will take to complete the commissioned work.

- A short sample piece will be written initially, to make sure you are happy with the style of writing. Once this has been discussed with you and approved, the work will continue.

- Our quote includes time allocated for the original writing, together with all reasonable re-writes, changes and editing.

- Should an unexpected number of changes or a large amount of re-writing be requested, over and above the original brief, we will notify you when the original time quoted for has been used up. We will then discuss with you any further charges which might be incurred, over and above the original quote.

The outcome of expectations not met is exasperation.

Chapter Twenty-One: Expectations and Enjoyment

How much you enjoy any experience or purchase, is directly related to what you have been led to expect.

We've looked at expectations and the frustrations and exasperations that can arise when you use the services of an outside professional, on a business to business basis. Equally (if not more) impactful on your pocket is how you manage communication when it's business to consumer.

You're selling a product or a service and this covers a huge spectrum, but whether you're providing pet food or party planning; photography or fishing equipment; baking classes or building projects; the one thing they all have in common is managing customer expectation and managing it well.

A Fine Line

It goes without saying that the practical and customer service side of your operation is important - delivering what you're going to deliver when you say you are; accurate description of products and services; prompt responses to queries; the ease of use and functionality of your website; the consistency and quality of what you're offering; the fact that the smallest of jobs gets as much attention as the largest, because we all know, from little acorns grow long-lasting and loyal clients.

But prior to all the above, and first and foremost, is the way you communicate what you're offering. And this isn't always straightforward. There's a fine line between making your products or services sound as excellent as they are, without eulogising to the extreme and setting yourself up for a fall, because expectations you've put in place can't be met.

Balancing your way along that fine line isn't easy and I have up-close and personal experience of this. One of my previous businesses was compiling and publishing an annual Hotel, Country Inn and B&B directory for people holidaying in America, along with providing a complimentary advisory, planning and booking service.

Naturally, there are always going to be one or two clients who might best be described as tricky, when it comes to planning a holiday. They're the ones who, placed on a cloud in heaven, would instantly complain the angel next door, was playing the harp too loudly. Accepting that, is part and parcel of running your business. I had one client who always took a pair of white cotton gloves on holidays, for running over various surfaces in hotel rooms to check for dust (I know, me neither!) We organised several trips for her over the years and she invariably reported back on her return - I was just thankful she never had cause to come to my house.

With the exception of a few oddities, most clients were a pleasure to deal with but intrinsic to that, was the provision by us of spot-on information and communication. Accommodations we worked with ranged from the smallest most intimate B&Bs to the largest most luxurious resorts and took in everything between, and whilst most people know what to expect from a Sheraton or a Marriott, many guests were looking for a completely different experience. We had to make sure that experience met expectation, at the same time as accurately extolling the attractions of each individual property in the book.

Rabbits

The text written for each hotel or inn, at the same time as being delightfully descriptive, totally tempting and specifically detailed, had to highlight any idiosyncrasies which guests might or might not love. An example, was a beautiful country inn in Vermont, where the theme was rabbits. It was a highly rated inn, with a brilliant location, fabulous views, acclaimed food, lovely innkeepers and cuddly toy rabbits of all shapes and sizes - everywhere. It was a Marmite experience, and we had to make that clear, ensure people who booked, were cuddly rabbit lovers not loathers.

Below is an excerpt from the introduction to the accommodation directory, to give you an idea of the text and tone we used to tackle the dual purpose of pulling some people in and warning others off, so choices they made, were right for them. This approach can be applied to your own business writing, should you have similar issues when it comes to information supplied to your clients.

Welcome to Selected Hotels & Inns

We believe the definition of a good holiday is one where expectations are met and hopefully exceeded. There is a vast range of choice as to where you stay on your trip, with differences between Resorts, Full-Service Hotels, Boutique Hotels, Country Inns and B&Bs. We thought, having presented you with so many options, the least we could do was start you off with some general background information.

The charm of smaller establishments is their size, informality and intimacy, although you'll find some services and facilities aren't automatically available. There may be no-one to help with your luggage at check-in, rooms may not have wi-fi and there isn't 24-hour room service. If you have a heavy case and a bad back, need to be in contact with the outside world and are subject to food cravings in the middle of the night, this isn't for you. On the other hand, if you travel light, never want to hear from the office again and can struggle through from a Cordon Bleu, five-course candlelit dinner to a gourmet breakfast without a midnight snack, you'll have a wonderful visit.

Small inns and many B&Bs offer great opportunities for guests to socialise; over breakfast or pre-dinner drinks, or perhaps eating breakfast, family-style with everyone seated round one table. This, for some people is a highlight of the holiday. But if you want to commune with nothing more than the scenery, each other and some excellent food, you might be happier at a larger establishment with less socialising and more solitude.

Some Boutique Hotels and Country Inns cater for children, some don't. Do take note and not offence at this. Telling you in advance is just as much for your benefit as for the owner's. Few parents find it relaxing if their boisterous toddler wreaks havoc with the antiques and throws-up on the priceless Persian rug.

As a rule, hoteliers and innkeepers are a warm, professional, friendly and helpful bunch – if they weren't, they wouldn't last long in the hospitality business. They are as keen for you to enjoy your trip as you are, so don't forget to mention if you have allergies, dietary requirements or don't want to tackle three flights of stairs. The same applies if you happen to have a phobia of any kind. Too late when greeted by four enthusiastically affectionate Great Danes, to mention you're terrified of dogs.

We hope we've given you a bit of background, but please don't hesitate to call our office for a chat. Not only do we have personal knowledge and client feedback on every single place we recommend, we're also great advice providers and specialists in helping you put together exactly the right trip.

Holiday planning should always be a pleasure, never a pain.

Chapter Twenty-Two: Don't Lose Your Balance

Waving or drowning?

Most businesses are launched by entrepreneurs and these are people who tend to think differently from others. Their ideas tend to not run in a linear way from A to B but might veer straight to N, maybe stopping off at F on the way, before heading back to C.

Concepts are always leaping out at them, and they're brilliant at seeing niches others have failed to spot. But the first set of innovative ideas that launches the business, is only the beginning, because the entrepreneurial mind never stops, it's always adding a *'What if . . . ?'* And a *'Why couldn't we . . .?'*

Entrepreneurs are the lifeblood of business. But every yin needs a yang, every entrepreneur needs someone who does think in straight lines, who wouldn't dream of being diverted by an N or an F until they'd securely sorted and signed off A, B and C. In a successful business, the person with the ability to keep two feet on the ground, a firm finger on the financial pulse and an eagle eye on day to day operation, is as invaluable as the bright ideas generator. Too many ideas, given their head, without a certain amount of practicality and pragmatism in the mix, create a seriously flawed business structure.

Tiger, Tiger Burning Bright

What many, somewhat astonished entrepreneurs have found, is that in successfully bringing their great ideas to life, they've created a tiger which they're now holding tightly by the tail. What's been grown (and let's not hesitate to mix a metaphor or several) is a massive mushroom on one thin stalk, and that one thin stalk is the entrepreneur who then finds him or herself running all aspects of the business, and some of them not well. But by this stage, they're so busy hanging tightly on to the tiger, there's no time to put in place the people and procedures needed for a well-balanced business, not to mention a well-balanced business person.

Waving not Drowning

As you define where you are with your business, it may help to think about the above. Picture the tiger (or the mushroom) and think ahead. You're fine, as long as you're still waving, but there may come a moment when that wave suddenly becomes something altogether more frantic. Ideally you want to pre-empt that moment, but if you've gone way past and are reading this, acknowledge it now and see if you can put some plans and actions in place to rectify.

Things to Think On

What, you may ask, does all of this have to do with copywriting? Well, as I think I've muttered before, every single part of your business is interwoven with and integral to every other part. If you're struggling with one thing, you're going to be struggling with others and struggling impedes clear thinking and clarity of communication. If that's impeded, then so is your business.

Done to Death

The work/life balance issue has been debated by cleverer and wiser minds than mine, and it's not as if it comes as a revelation – we're not stupid, we know what we should be doing, but like exercise and cutting down on chocolate, it's easier said than done.

Talking about balance isn't self-indulgent, it's business and self-survival. There are only so many poles on which you can keep plates spinning, and by the time they start thumping down on your head – you've left it too late. Whilst effective time management is a whole different subject, a book on its own, it never hurts to stop, look around and see things from a different angle with a practical perspective.

*Creating something is just the start,
as Dr. Frankenstein found, you have to know how to handle it.*

133

Chapter Twenty-Three: Public Speaking Or Root Canal Treatment?

Capturing an Audience.

Statistically, public speaking apparently ranks higher in stress terms than almost any other activity. Quite what the parameters were for research that produced this startling fact, I'm not sure. I find it hard to believe that addressing an audience could cause more angst than say a visit to a man in a mask who runs out of the room whilst zapping you with x-rays, before returning to do things with a needle and drill.

However, there is no doubt, that whilst there are those who love nothing better than a captive audience, the reactions of others range from it being a minor chore to a knee-knocking, sweaty palmed endurance test. And let's not forget, before you stand up to give that speech or presentation, you're faced with the task of writing it.

These are a few practical tips which might make both writing and delivery a little less painful.

Audience Pleaser Pointers

- Keep it reasonably brief. When it comes to a speech, shorter's safer.

- Under no circumstances start your speech with '*A is for* . . . this induces a dreadful sense of foreboding in your audience who see where you're going, and promptly lose the will to live, let alone listen.

- Try and start with a small witticism, at the same time remembering you're not there as a stand-up. And when I say a small joke, I mean it, there's a time for a shaggy dog tale and this isn't it. Which brings us to another important point . . .

- Speak slowly. SLOWLY and CLEARLY. If you gabble, you breathe more rapidly. Rapid breathing leads to swifter inhaling and although an indrawn breath is normally no problem, up close and personal with a microphone, it can sound truly alarming.

- Whilst your breathing should never be too rapid, try not to go to the other extreme and forget about it altogether. Omitting to take a breath can lead to dizziness, and sustained swaying results in audience consternation, with people more focused on whether you're going to fall over, than on anything you're saying.

- Body language is important. Raised shoulders are a sign of tension and it's a known fact, when people are watching you, many of them will unconsciously mimic your movements. Bearing in mind, most of us aren't swan-necked at the best of times, think how a roomful of ears on shoulders is going to look. Do everyone a favour, shake those shoulders down.

- If you're the slightest bit nervous, don't hold your notes. Rest them safely and securely on the table or podium in front of you. The sight of a shivering sheaf of papers does not shout confidence.

- Even if you're not unduly nervous, your body will still probably react to the situation with a shot of adrenaline, putting you in a fight or flight mode. This was handy back in the ice-age, snout to snout with a sabre tooth, but is possibly superfluous to requirements in the current situation, ignore it as much as you can.

- An adrenaline rush can give you a dry mouth, so don't be alarmed if you find your lips suddenly sticking firmly to your teeth. Casually take a sip from your handy, pre-placed glass of water, bearing in mind you need to pause properly to swallow. Failure to do this can lead to embarrassing coughing, choking and lots of people keen to practice the Heimlich Manoeuvre.

- A glass of wine may well help relax you prior to your speaking slot, but know your limitations. Sliding gently under the table, five minutes before you're introduced, won't work wonders for your reputation.

- Ensure you're dressed appropriately. Not as silly as it sounds, on several levels. We know what a difference appearance makes, and have probably all had nightmares of something going horribly adrift. But even if everything stays exactly where it should, it's got to look good too. We all have outfits that make us feel a million dollars, along with costly mistakes that make us look like a cross between the Hunchback of Notre Dame and Dracula's mum on a bad day. Stick with the million-dollar option.

- Finally, don't forget to look up, make eye contact and smile, smile, smile. Most people are instinctively polite, they'll smile back and you'll all feel better, even if your speech is truly dreadful.

I would also add a cautionary note to those who, like me, are vertically challenged. I once gave a talk at a hospitality industry conference in America where, standing behind the podium, meant only the very top of my head could be seen by the audience. The event organisers speedily provided a sturdy wooden box on which I could stand. The ideal solution. All went well until, in the enthusiasm of the presentation, I took a sideways step, I'll say no more.

Rest assured, behind a podium, no-one can see your knees knocking.

Chapter Twenty-Four: Writing Your Own Business Book

Oh no I can't! Oh yes you can!

The definition of a business book? In my view, something that's written to enhance and add an extra dimension to whatever it is you do to earn your living.

Writing a book on your own area of expertise can be a boost for both your profile and your profits. There's no doubt It adds gravitas to your professional image and please don't tell me you don't know what you'd say, because you're going to be writing on a subject you know inside and out – your own area of expertise.

A book gives you a tangible product to sell which can generate an ongoing passive income, even if sales aren't enormous. It gives you a great hook to use for press releases as well as for publicity on social media, and what you produce certainly doesn't have to be the size of War and Peace - in fact I'd specifically advise against that.

Authoring a book gives you extra authority in your field, offers opportunity to give talks, hold workshops and be invited to take part in panel discussions - all of which are further chances to promote both your business and your book. I think everyone who's done it would agree, it adds a hefty extra string to your bow and none of us can turn our noses up at that.

Routes to Publication

As you'll know, publishing has changed radically in recent past years, presenting you with what can seem like a bewildering range of options. You may choose to go down the traditional route which involves finding a literary agent to represent you. If they're good at what they do, they'll fly your flag for you, know the right publishers to approach and hopefully negotiate a good deal.

On the other hand, you may prefer to put yourself directly in front of a specialist publisher, marketing to a receptive readership - for example, the health and well-being market. If this doesn't appeal, you might opt for self or independent publishing which gives you freedom to produce exactly the book you want. If you publish independently you can choose to initially put it out there as an ebook which is not a large investment at all. However, If you have a showroom, shop or are giving talks, you may find it to your advantage to have a certain amount of hard copies to hand because you'll have the opportunity to sell them directly.

When is a Book Not a Book

We're talking about books, but in this digital age with different formats and platforms, your information could just as well be written as a script for a podcast, a download, a webinar, a series of webinars or indeed recorded for YouTube. The only thing all these options have in common is that the writing needs to be engaging, coherent, informative and tailored to the audience who are most likely to read, view or hear it. So, whilst there are lots of clever people who know their way round a platform and can sort you out from that point of view, the original information does need to originate with you.

Different Models

There are as many reasons for writing a book, ranging from the intensely personal to the purely commercial, as there are different ways of going about it. Your book might be self-funding; self-help; health related; inspirational or for training purposes. It may be a recounting of your own experiences or a subject that's cathartic for you to write about and empowering for others to read:

- **Self-Funding**: It goes without saying, this is a great route to take, but of course, only works if you're in a business where others are prepared to spend money with you because your book will promote them and is guaranteed to reach a wide audience. It's probably more accurate to call something like this a directory, or a register and an example might be a book that features write-ups and detailed information on hotels or restaurants.

- **Self-Help**: Perennially popular, because there's not one of us who doesn't think life might be so much better if we could only find and follow the right set of advice and instructions. Time management; stress management; business management; parenting methods; decluttering your home; re-organising your work/life balance - there are very few subjects, commercial or domestic, on which people couldn't do with some input and are happy to buy a book to get it.

- **Health Related**: As a nutritionist, a trainer or an alternative therapist, you almost certainly have a lot of practical information and suggestions for a healthier life-style, whether via diet, exercise or a better understanding of physiology and metabolism.

- **Life-style:** Florist? Garden Designer? Caterer? Baker? Interior designer? How much do we all love what you might have to tell us? But it's all been said before, I hear you shriek, to which I'd say, well that's true but does that affect in any way its continuing popularity? Does yet another tv cookery or gardening show detract from any of the others? The fact is, every single one of you has your own voice, your own approach your own tricks, hints and tips of the trade and your own unique approach to what you do.

- **Inspirational**: Still focusing on the fact that we all want to feel better, something as simple and straightforward as an inspirational short story or poem for every day of the year, can and has in the past, proved incredibly powerful, popular and lucrative.

- **Training:** Slipping smoothly from the spiritual to the practical - a well-written book, by an expert who knows their subject inside out, is always welcome. If, for example, you're an IT guru, able to take people through the intricacies and mysteries of various computer programmes, you'd be providing an invaluable source of succour to a lot of struggling technophobes.

- **Cathartic:** Sometimes a book needs to be written because of experiences in your life and it can be as cathartic for you, as it is beneficial to those who read it. I've had the pleasure of working with those who initially had no intention of writing for anyone but themselves, but then created a piece of work that cried out to be shared, which in turn has led to successful and inspiring speaking careers.

- **Experiences:** This is not an instruction or training book, but about adventures and misadventures within your own particular profession. After all, look what his books did for James Herriot.

Excuses for Not Writing

- *'I can't write.'* Well, I can only refer you back to Chapter 2!

- *'I can't find the time.'* Well of course you can't find the time, when did anybody ever trip over some unexpected spare time? If you're running your own business there aren't ever enough hours in the day, but spare time is a misnomer. Spare time is when you put your feet up, read a good book and sip gently from a glass of something intoxicating. Writing a book doesn't remotely come into the same category. A book could turn out to be as important to your business as your website or your level of customer service satisfaction.

- **'I don't have the faintest idea how to go about it.'** Oh, but you do, because you'd approach this the same way you approach all the other things you do. Are you a born planner and love nothing more than mulling over a mind map? Or maybe you're a fan of little yellow stickies on the wall? Perhaps you're devoted to differently coloured sharpies and a chart, or maybe you're a seat-of-the-pants person, confident the pieces will fall into perfect place as you go along? There are as many different ways to approach a book project as there are books written. Whether it's a factual business book or fantastic fiction – simply charge at it in the same way you attack everything else. Have faith in your own common sense, ability and methods of working. If they've brought you this far in your business, why would they let you down now?

- **'I wouldn't know what to say.'** Again, I'd have to strongly disagree (am I stroppy, or what?). When you talk to a new customer or client you take them through exactly what it is you can offer them. You almost certainly don't have a script for this, it's all in your head. It's automatic, because you know what you're doing, as well as precisely what you want to tell them. I'd also lay bets that you spend a great deal of your time talking about your business, thinking about your business, addressing issues that crop up in your business, talking to colleagues about your business and putting plans in place for your business. So, truth be told, there's an awful lot of stuff all ready and waiting to be written about.

- **'I wouldn't know where to start.'** It doesn't matter where you start - at the end, in the middle, with a list of contents, by introducing yourself, or just with a whole series of notes jotted down as thoughts occur to you. The important thing is not where you start, but simply to make a start.

If you know who you are and who you're talking to, you'll know what to say!

Chapter Twenty-Five: Illusion / Disillusion

Between perception and reality there's a surprisingly large chasm, from which can arise any number of knotty problems . . .

. . . Sherlock Holmes and Doctor Watson are spending the night in a tent, they wake in the middle of the night and Holmes says,

'Watson, what do you see?' Watson, in reflective mood, says,

'Well, I look up and I see the infinity of the sky, the clarity of the crescent moon and a million points of light as the stars shine coldly down upon us. What is it you see?' and Holmes says,

'Somebody's stolen the bloody tent!'

It's a daft joke, but also a neat illustration of how two people see the same thing differently - which is why and how, even the most carefully crafted communication can sometimes miss its mark. It's essential to take various angles into consideration when creating copy, and getting into the habit of doing that will change the way you see and identify business opportunities or threats.

Looking at Competition

Is competition good or bad? Well, it can go either way. Most of us have it and whilst it may well make us want to throw our toys out of the pram, it's not a bad thing. It certainly makes it a lot easier to categorise yourself, because people are already aware of your type of business. If, on the other hand, you're unique in what you do without a whiff of a competitor, there are obvious advantages. But the other side of the coin is that people aren't instantly able to align and identify you with something familiar, so your business message has to have even more of the clarity I'm always banging on about.

Where there is competition it's always good to see what, in your opinion, they're doing right or on the other hand, not doing quite so well. And it's always sensible to keep an eye on the level of fees being charged, so you know whether or not your own charges are in the right ball park.

When looking at the fees though, bear in mind the *Best Of* ranges sold by most supermarkets. Proven consumer psychology shows people are often prepared to pay a higher price for what they are assured is a better product. So many of us are happy to load our baskets without really knowing whether we're actually paying for better quality or just clever marketing.

This perception principle applies particularly well to food, because our stomachs are close to our hearts, and as far as budget permits, we're anxious to get the best for our families and ourselves. But it's actually relevant to all businesses. Think carefully when setting your fees and be aware that sometimes, pricing yourself well below your competitors to draw in more clients, has the opposite effect. For example, if people are coming to you as a practising osteopath, specialising in back pain, they don't want to muck around, they're in dire straits, they want help, they want relief and they want it quickly. It may be a false assumption on their part that by opting for a practice charging higher fees, they'll receive better treatment – but sometimes that's just human nature, isn't it?

A Shoulder on Which to Lean

I think it's helpful to liaise with and build relationships with others in the same business as you. It's handy to know there's someone on whom you can rely, should you need to pass along any work in the event of illness or overload. It may be that they specialise in an area of the business which you don't and vice versa, leading to an alliance which can be profitable and mutually beneficial. Additionally, and sometimes far more importantly, they'll instantly be able to empathise and sympathise with any profession-specific problems you might encounter along the way and can often offer sage advice.

Never forget though, your unique selling point is you, don't be tempted to ape anyone else, however much you admire what they're doing and how they're doing it, you risk losing your edge, your authenticity and your way.

Pitfalls of Perfection

Professional pride's a great thing and vital to your success. It can also be darn difficult to handle, particularly when writing for your own business. This is because no piece is ever perfect, it can always be improved, a sentence tweaked, a word changed there, a phrase added here. When it comes to writing, the only thing you can be 100% certain of, is that the moment you see it in print, your critically eagle eye will land on something you could have done better.

The only advice I can offer is whilst perfection's preferable, it's not always possible. Don't beat yourself up about it.

Is Bigger Better?

We all love nothing better than acquiring a client or customer with a big name and a hefty budget and we know a prestigious client often leads to other equally prestigious clients, which is all to the good. You may hold the view that the bigger the client the better, but the other side of the coin is that the bigger the client, the bigger the client-shaped hole they leave, should they decide to move on to pastures new.

I'd never suggest you don't aim as high as you can, but I wonder whether the perception of success resting only on the biggest names and budgets, can be a risky assumption. It's probably safer to spread your net wide enough to include clients of all shapes and sizes, it certainly gives you a more secure base, and secure and successful certainly aren't mutually exclusive.

I think It's important when writing or talking about your business to strike a happy balance. You don't want to scare off the big boys by coming across as a cottage industry, on the other hand, you don't want to put the wind up any smaller or newly launching businesses, who might make an incorrect assumption that your fees will be beyond their reach.

Change of Mind

I've said it before, and here I am, saying it again (well I never promised there'd be no repetition did I?) Perceptions and impressions are formed incredibly swiftly, which is why your language, approach and message need to be immediately understood.

If you're the slightest bit sceptical how swiftly the brain works, and the vast difference in understanding a tiny shift in focus can make, there's no better example than what you're looking at now:

Still sceptical?

Chapter Twenty-Six: Leaping Off The Page

Get text right and it leaps off the page, get it wrong and it lies there limply.

Writing a piece of text in a different and sometimes unexpected way can instantly create character for a business, just as it can for an individual. It can make you jump out from amongst competitors, immediately hooking and holding interest, because you're different. But what's written, will only work, if it feels right for you.

When you write for yourself your text will, of course, be authentic provided you let yourself go and follow your instinct. However, if, as can sometimes happen to any of us, your instinct seems to have taken a leave of absence and you need to call on some outside help, make sure you're comfortable with the style of what they produce. If you're not thrilled – say so, because the text is presenting and representing you and your company. If you're not comfortable with the way it's doing that, then it's not the right text.

As an example, of how stand-out character can be created, have a wander through the texts below. One's for a marketing flyer, the other for a networking elevator pitch. Option 1 in each case is a straighter, more formal presentation, Option 2 is probably more commercial because it uses humour, and might be likely to linger longer in people's minds. The most important deciding factor though is, if this was your business and your presentation, which would you be most comfortable with?

- **Option 1**

AURORA FITNESS

Gym facilities, Body Toning, Personalised Fitness Plans

We're a well-established ladies-only gym and we provide a wide range of

fitness services to clients including:

30 Minute Workouts

Weight Loss & Nutritional Advice

Body Toning

Circuit Training

Fitness Plans

We're open to ladies of any age and all walks of life.

Here at Aurora, we understand the concept of client satisfaction and rely on client recommendations, so, we're always improving our services.

Contact us to take the first steps to improving your health and well-being.

~

- **Option 2**

AURORA FITNESS

The Gym with its Sneakers on the Ground!

Given the choice, what would you prefer to wrap yourself around,

would it be an exercise machine, or a chocolate éclair?

If you murmured éclair, think leotards should be made illegal and believe sweat looks better on a horse, then we're talking to you.

You may be feeling guilty about your ongoing health and fitness, but not quite guilty enough to have done anything about it yet, perhaps we can help.

We are a gym, but not as you know it. We're ladies-only, all ages, shapes, sizes and degrees of determination. We offer weight loss programmes, personal fitness plans and sensible nutrition advice, but we're the least bossy people you'll ever meet, our 30-minute work-outs are mercifully brief and we have a lot of fun.

Come and see for yourself. Start feeling good, not guilty.

Aurora Fitness, the gym for women who hate gyms. Call for a chat.

~

- **Option 1**

Elevator Pitch for an Internal Financial Planning Manager

My name is Helen Watts and I'm a Financial Planning Manager. My job is to help people with their finances and offer impartial advice. I work with commercial enterprises and individual customers, to assist them with their business financing, personal investments, retirement funds, estate and tax planning and any other matters that come within my area of expertise.

The bank makes no charge for this service and I am on a salary, so when advising you, there is no commission involved. I would very much enjoy talking to you to see if I can help with your business or personal financial planning. Please don't hesitate to contact me and I would welcome referrals to anyone else you know who needs help with their financial planning. Again, my name is Helen Watts and I'm a Financial Planning Manager.

~

- **Option 2**

  ### Elevator Pitch for an Internal Financial Planning Manager

  I'm Helen Watts, and if you're someone who turns pale and clammy at the mention of Financial Planning, don't panic.

  Yes, I do talk money, but I also offer a listening ear, coffee, smelling salts if needed and only as much advice on your business financing or personal investments as you're ready to hear. We can also, if you're up to it, touch lightly on retirement thoughts and look at the estate and tax planning side of things.

  My advice is completely unbiased, because the nice people at the bank insist on paying me a salary, so commission considerations don't arise. I hope I've reassured you that putting a few financial safeguards in place might not be such an unsettling experience after all, and might even put your mind to rest on a few things. I look forward to chatting to you and anyone else you know who also fears a funny turn when it comes to talking finance, I'm Helen Watts, taking the pain out of planning.

  ~

  *People may not need you immediately,
  but make yourself memorable and they'll contact you
  when they do.*

Chapter Twenty-Seven: Stop The Blogging, I Want To Get Off

Blogging's like any relationship – don't get involved unless you're ready to commit.

If you're pushed for time, and who isn't – outsourcing time-consuming tasks makes sense, particularly if it's a task you don't like doing. Something you don't like doing, invariably takes twice as long as something you do, and giving it to someone else means you'll spend far less time swearing and banging your head against the nearest solid object.

Blogging about your business is a brilliant way of raising your profile, but it does require commitment, consistency and planning, although none of those are insurmountable so long as you set yourself realistic targets. However, unless you're incredibly prolific, with an awfully large amount of ever-changing information to impart, a weekly blog may turn out to be a little over-ambitious, and there's a fine line between profile-raising and boring. You want your target audience to be turned on, not off so only you can decide what's going to work best for you - fortnightly, monthly, quarterly, annually?

And, without wishing to be a party pooper, even if you're getting someone else to blog for you, you're not off the hook. You still need to convey to your writer what you want them to tell your readers. Your writer, in turn has to know enough about your business, your message and your personality, to be able to slip easily into your shoes and make the text read authentically.

Lisa Wainwright is a counsellor and hypnotherapist who specialises in working with teenagers. Her monthly blogs speak mainly to parents. Lisa is a warm but reserved personality, an expert in listening and hearing what individuals need from her. Her instructions are that once a month, she will provide half a page of notes on the subject she wants to blog about.

Rather than writing as an expert in her field, she prefers to come across as a parent with whom other parents can easily identify. She prefers to establish a relationship of equals, rather than sounding like a lecturing professional. Below is the sort of thing I'd suggest for her.

Lisa Wainwright's Blog:

A Change of Direction

I stopped for a coffee yesterday between meetings and was at a table next to a group of chatting and joking teenagers, they were young 13 or 14 I'd say, and it was impossible not to hear their conversation. They were, unsurprisingly, on their phones and comparing pictures, speculating how much filtering had gone into those of celebrities and of other people they knew. I had to restrain myself from leaning over and suggesting sharply, it wouldn't hurt if they were a little kinder in their observations and comments.

Insufferably interfering of me? Yes of course it would have been, and of course I didn't do it. But I finished my coffee and left feeling depressed. So many of our kids struggle to attain what's held up as ideal - the perfect body, the perfect weight, the perfect image, the perfect pout – but what they're trying to emulate isn't real. The honed, toned, buffed, tanned, dieted to distraction - and let's not even mention photo-shopped - models and celebrities we see, they're not real-life any more than Harry Potter. Why is it that our young people, who've hoovered up and loved the Potter books knowing darn well they're not going to be picking up a magic wand any time soon, can't see how equally make-believe are the images they struggle to emulate?

Eating disorders amongst both girls and boys are on the rise and we shouldn't be surprised. Because when you're trying to measure up to the impossible, that's precisely what it is and is always going to be – impossible! So, how to best to help our kids? How to counteract images that have so little connection with reality? My personal conviction is we may not be able to change society as a whole, but if we can change enough individuals then Hey Presto (or would it be Expelliarmus?) maybe we can head in a kinder direction. I know from talking to so many of you, you agree our job as parents is to try and instil enough self-confidence and worth into our young, to let them make their own realistic assessment as to what's normal, healthy and makes sense as opposed to what isn't and doesn't.

Obviously, a subject for further discussion, debate and input but, if we can get this even a little bit right, we'll be giving them wings, permission to soar and who knows, perhaps to make their own magic!

As always, you know I welcome your comments, thoughts and approaches and in the meantime, I promise to behave better in coffee shops.

~

Kate Dartington runs a bookkeeping business and deals (highly efficiently) with issues such as credit chasing and daily admin for her clients. She works with newly launched as well as established small businesses.

She's dynamic, excellent at what she does and doesn't hold back on chivvying when figures are overdue or administering a virtual kick up the bottom, where she feels it's necessary. She runs a smooth operation, with an ever-growing base of grateful (well-trained) clients who think she is God's gift to their business.

Kate wants a blog to go out as part of her quarterly newsletter which otherwise comprises updates and facts and figures relevant to the companies she deals with. She wants to soften the factual stuff with some personal input. She knows she's bossy, but that's what she's built her reputation on and she doesn't mind trading on it.

Kate Dartington's Blog

Books and Covers

We probably shouldn't judge a book by its cover. We shouldn't make snap judgements. But let's be honest, most of us do, although in this instance I'm not talking about books but about businesses – your business to be exact.

We know there's absolutely no guarantee that a sleekly designed, glossily beautiful, top-quality business card is going to provide a service or product that fulfils its promise, but it is more likely to get your foot in the door than a card that just doesn't cut it. Should we put our faith in glossy, well-presented business material as opposed to that obviously produced on a wing and a prayer? No. Do we? Yes, a lot of the time that's exactly what we do. Appearances and impressions count. You wouldn't turn up at a business meeting in torn jeans, flip-flops and a ripped tee-shirt, because the way you look, is important. It's equally important your business looks good.

I know a lot of you are muttering right now about tight budgets and I'm well aware of how tight a budget can be. But presenting yourself cheaply is a false economy. Think about the things people might see first - your business card, your website, a brochure? If you can stretch to a graphic designer to put together a professional logo, that's the way you should go.

If you can't stretch, then stick to something simple and professional. Go for the best quality card you can afford and don't, please don't, be seduced by economies of scale! Yes, if you order a couple of thousand it certainly works out cheaper per card than going for a 100. On the other hand, there are always going to be things you want to change as you move forward. You're far better off ordering fewer cards and using them than having to chuck loads away – because then, they won't have worked out more reasonably at all.

One last, but not least, suggestion. Even if you're economising on your cards, always spend that little bit extra to remove any advertising the print company want to include. True, by including their ad, you get the cards cheaper, or even free, but *Printed Free by A. N. Other Printers* never ever makes you look good!

~

Below is an example of the sort of blog I put out although – and isn't this the very height of hypocrisy (although I've always suggested you should do what I say, not what I do!), they don't go out as often as they should.

I've deliberately tended to make these quite stylised and personal and not particularly business-centred, because that's very much part of my brand.

Create Communication Blog

Woman or Wuss?

Been putting off a cholesterol test for ages. Woman or wuss? Over the years have not behaved well, when presented with someone in white who wants to take blood. There are phlebotomists all over London, who've dealt with me and are still in counselling. However, challenges are for rising to. Swallow a couple of paracetamol on a pain preventative basis, and present myself at the local surgery. They've installed a system for patients to register their arrival which proves slightly problematic – it's a touch screen, but hands are shaking so badly, keep missing aimed-for icon.

Take my place in waiting room and have an unobtrusive swig or two of Rescue Remedy. Have also taken precaution of bringing cooling menthol stick used for headaches, in the hopes it might prevent me from coming over all unnecessary. In updating the surgery, they've also installed a loudspeaker to alert the next patient. Can't help but feel it could do with a bit of adjusting, it's way beyond a healthy decibel level and every time it sounds, an entire waiting room full of people jump as one. Hope there's nobody in with a weak heart. Woman next to me wants to talk. I don't, so feign strong interest in hastily grabbed leaflet which turns out, embarrassingly, to be on STDs. We all jump a few more times then I'm summoned, although not easy to walk whilst knocking back the rest of the Rescue Remedy, scrubbing forehead with 4Head and scrunching up STD leaflet.

Phlebotomist takes one look at me and can tell she's got a right one here, 'Goodness,' she says, flinching as a wave of menthol from the 4Head hits her. 'That's strong stuff. Teeny bit nervous, are we?' Concede I am indeed a teeny bit nervous and say I hope she isn't. We laugh, and she gets busy with the black rubber tubing. 'Just relax,' she says. Relax? Relax is something you do on the sofa with the tv on, not what you do when a woman who can't see straight because of menthol in her eyes, is looking where to stick her needle.

'There, all done, not so bad, was it? Just press down firmly.' I nod and rise, then descend again swiftly as room starts to spin. 'Not to worry,' I say, euphoric with the fact it's over 'Always happens, will just stick head between knees for a moment or two.'

Half an hour, three glasses of water and two and a half faints later, make my way home. Had planned to write a rather complicated but vital business plan for a restaurant client this afternoon. Might just leave it till tomorrow – think that would be in his best interests.

~

There's no end to the changes that can be wrought by writing.

Chapter Twenty-Eight: Dark And Stormy

Clichés become clichés for good reason – they work.

As I've said (feel free to add, ad nauseam!) the tone and voice of your business and the image you project are so important, because your website, your brochure, your business card or your social media output may be the first contact potential clients have with you. You want them to like you, you want them to like your business and it's never ever too early to start building a relationship.

The ways you can present yourself are many and varied, depending on who you are and who you're talking to. To demonstrate how simply and swiftly the whole *feel* of a piece of text can be changed, I'm going to chuck some further ideas into the pot, by looking at *Dark and Stormy.* That may sound a little cracked, I know, but hang on in there and you'll see where I'm going with this.

'It was a dark and stormy night.' . . .

. . . is the opening sentence used by English novelist Edward Bulwer-Lytton in his 1830 novel Paul Clifford. It's been heartily derided as purple prose, florid, melodramatic and clichéd, although I must confess, I'm more than fond of a well-turned cliché, simply because it's always completely clear and instantly understood.

However, in 1982 that line gave rise to the *Bulwyer-Lytton Fiction Contest*, still held today, where writers compete to create the most dreadful opening lines. Mind you, I can't help but think old Edward B-L has had the last and loudest laugh – after all, whose name is universally known now?

I've written some short pieces below. Each of these start with that same sturdy wording, but then lead you down a completely different path, showing how much flexibility you have when it comes to changes in tone and expectation.

Romance

It was a dark and stormy night, and busy battling the unrelenting wind with her umbrella, she wasn't looking when she stepped off the curb into a puddle of massive proportions. Her heel twisted under her as she tried to avoid the unexpected soaking, and she would have fallen, had it not been for a sudden firm arm round her waist.

~

Horror

It was a dark and stormy night, and there had been yet another power cut. She hated being on her own in that house where every mirror threw back an unexpectedly angled image and every movement, a floor creak. It was odd then that she should feel reassured, for just a second or so, when a hand slipped into hers.

~

Thriller

It was a dark and stormy night, he liked it that way. He had his work to do and it was work best done privately. On a night like this, people had their heads down, weren't watching. But he was. Watching was what he was particularly good at, and it didn't take him long to find her. The next one.

~

Science Fiction

It was a dark and stormy night when Ben heard the tap, tap, tapping on the window. He wasn't frightened, he was eight years old and ready for anything. He pulled back the curtains his mother had drawn earlier. Outside the window, and how odd was that, because he was on the first floor, was another little boy, with his eyes closed. Then he opened them. And Ben could see, this really wasn't another little boy at all.

~

Comedy

It was a dark and stormy night and Oscar was as reluctant to go for a walk as she was to take him. She opted for letting him out in the garden but wuss that he was, he refused to proceed unaccompanied. She'd pulled

169

the back door closed to keep in the heat, before she remembered it was nearly as temperamental as Oscar, with a tendency to warp in the damp. She pushed, it was indeed stuck. She pushed harder, and Oscar whined softly behind her. She stepped back, trod on his paw, staggered sideways to avoid him and plunged clumsily into a planted patio pot. She felt like whining too.

~

When you're writing, you're like a tour guide, you can take people in any direction you want.

Chapter Twenty-Nine: A Final Word To The Wise

I should probably end this book with a gloriously inspirational quote, along with some positive affirmations to chant, as you pile on the £s. But I think you know me better than that by now.

I certainly hope though that some of the angles, thoughts and strategies I've been rambling on about, will boost your trust and confidence in your own excellent common sense and gut instincts, which can usually be relied upon to steer you in the right directions. And if, on the odd occasion they don't, I can only set before you, the example of the Fainting Goats.

This particular breed has an odd nervous-system quirk, when they have a fright, their muscles freeze, and they gently topple over. This method of dealing with the upsetting or unexpected, has always struck me as a useful coping mechanism to add to one's business tool-kit. Hit by a distressing setback, you might find it helpful to simply keel over and rest quietly and thoughtfully, until you're ready to deal with it.

~ end ~

Printed in Great Britain
by Amazon